THE MOST INCREDIBLE LAW ENFORCEMENT STORIES EVER TOLD

20 INSPIRING TRUE TALES OF HEROISM AND BRAVERY FROM REAL COPS

JONATHAN HUNT

CONTENTS

ATTENTION:

DO YOU WANT MY FUTURE BOOKS AT HEAVY DISCOUNTS AND EVEN FOR FREE?

HEAD OVER TO WWW.SECRETREADS.COM AND JOIN MY SECRET BOOK CLUB!

INTRODUCTION

Part of the job of being a police officer is always being ready to put your life on the line to save innocent civilians threatened by violent people or circumstances.

This book covers 20 real-life incidents in which police officers from around the world have done exactly that.

We'll cover the story of one officer who suffered severe burns when he climbed into a car that was ablaze with fire to save the people trapped inside and the story of the officer who sustained multiple stab wounds to stop a crazed mass killer from setting fire to a gas station.

We'll tell you about the officer who punched his way through ice in a frozen river in an attempt to save children trapped in the icy waters. And the one who risked his life and career to expose corruption in his department. Plus, another officer that used his own body as a cushion to save the life of a suicidal man who leaped from a multi-story building.

Each of the above stories, and the others that we'll cover in this book, are true and stark reminders of what police officers are often called upon to do.

Not every police officer will experience the same kinds of life-threatening situations that this book covers. But every police officer has to be prepared at a moment's notice.

One moment, a police officer can be performing their routine daily duties. The very next minute, they may be forced to take immediate action to stop a violent assailant or rescue people from a freezing river or an inferno of fire.

That's exactly what makes them heroes.

Let's get started.

CHAPTER ONE

DAVID MUNIZ

When we think of police officers, action-filled movies and TV shows about cops are what come to mind first for most of us. Movies and shows that deal with police officers commonly show characters in law enforcement routinely getting involved in shootouts and altercations with violent criminals on the streets or taking on heavily armed drug gangs.

For most police officers around the world, though, life on the job may be a little bit less exciting and action-packed than what we see in those kinds of movies and shows. Working as a police officer involves lots of paperwork, writing tickets, and other mundane and routine tasks.

However, every police officer who signs up still has to be prepared to act courageously and decisively in the line of duty if the situation ever arises. Every so often, police officers will be forced to confront violent criminals threatening the lives of others. In scenarios like this, law enforcement officers have no choice but to act.

But at the same time, it's also important for police officers to display good judgment and discernment. Being a police officer does not just give you a 'license to kill', and not every confrontation involving police and criminals armed with guns results in a big gunfight like we commonly see in movies or shows.

That's because, sometimes, an officer who finds themself in a deadly confrontation will elect to de-escalate a situation and talk down an assailant or a criminal. In the case of police officer David Muniz, this was something he did even after being shot directly in the chest..., even though he could more easily have returned fire and killed his opponent.

The incident occurred in Cleveland, Ohio in March 2015.

The start of that fateful day was just like any other for Officer Muniz. But everything changed when the Fourth District Police Station in Cleveland received a report from a distressed woman named Juliette Johnson.

Juliette claimed that her 64-year-old husband, Theodore, had been drinking excessively and was now drunk and waving a pistol around, threatening to kill both her and their landlady.

Muniz was the officer dispatched to the couple's apartment on Ottawa Avenue. Once there, he was met by the landlady, who directed him to the Johnson apartment.

For many police officers, this task was the exact kind of absolute nightmare that they rarely, if ever, encounter, but were trained to handle: enter the confined apartment of an unstable and violent man armed with a gun. Further complicating matters was that Theodore Johnson already had a domestic abuse conviction and a history of violent and drunk behavior.

Carefully, Muniz crept up the stairs to the location of the Johnson apartment.

"Police!" Muniz shouted as he slowly but steadily ascended the staircase with his duty pistol in hand.

The staircase now came to a corner. Rounding the corner, Muniz instantly encountered the armed Theodore, who was standing at the top of the staircase and fired twice down at Muniz.

One of the bullets missed and struck the wall, but the other bullet hit Muniz directly in the chest.

Muniz staggered backwards but managed to keep his balance. Miraculously, the bullet had been stopped by the bulletproof vest that he was wearing under his uniform. With the round lodged in his vest, Muniz aimed his pistol up at Theodore.

Many police officers in that situation would have returned fire instantly, and they would have had good cause to do so. In this case, having been fired upon first, Muniz would have been acting in self-defense had he returned fire.

But instead, Muniz elected to de-escalate the situation with Theodore. After shooting Muniz, Theodore lowered his pistol to his side.

"Kill me!" Theodore demanded.

"No," Muniz replied with his duty pistol aimed squarely at Theodore's torso, "we don't want to kill you. Just drop the gun."

"I want to die," Johnson insisted.

"No, you do not want to die," Muniz retorted.

Other police officers who were with Muniz appeared at this time and ascended the stairs. They were behind Muniz and likewise had their guns trained on Johnson.

"You can't help me," said Theodore, growing increasingly distraught, "shoot me! I shot you, shoot me!"

"I know you shot me," said Muniz. "But I'm not going to shoot you."

A few seconds that felt like minutes passed. Despite having every opportunity to drop his gun and end the confrontation peacefully, Theodore decided against taking Muniz up on his offer.

Theodore raised his gun, and Muniz and the other police officers were forced to open fire. Struck by multiple bullets, Johnson collapsed dead atop the staircase.

****

The incident gained widespread national attention. Initially, all that was released to the news media was that a Cleveland police officer shot and killed a man in his mid-60s in his apartment. Muniz and the other officers involved were also immediately put under investigation, first by the Cleveland Police Department and then by the Cuyahoga Sheriff's Department as well.

Muniz and the other officers were relegated to desk duties exclusively during the investigation period. It wasn't until seven months later that the body camera footage from the camera affixed to Muniz's uniform was released to end the investigation.

The footage proved that Muniz had acted with extreme patience in an attempt to de-escalate the situation peacefully even after being shot in the chest. This put to rest all doubts about his actions, and Muniz and the other officers were given Awards.

"These guys are absolutely genuine heroes," Steve Loomistold, the President of the Cleveland Police Patrolmen's Association, later said after the awards had been handed out.

The incident played into the national debate about the role of body camera technology within American law enforcement, specifically its role given the recent increase in crime.

Many politicians and people in the United States view body camera technology as necessary to either prevent or document instances of police brutality, particularly incidents involving fatalities. That's why police departments all over the United States started to equip their law enforcement officers with body camera footage around the mid-2010s.

Body camera technology may have documented instances of violent police brutality, but it has just as many (if not more so) documented instances of police heroism and restraint.

The confrontation between David Muniz and Theodore Johnson is a prime example of this. Immediately following the engagement, Muniz was suspected of having shot down Johnson without restraint and was subjected to intense scrutiny by the media, local law enforcement associations, and politicians across the United States.

But the footage proved that Muniz had acted with incredible restraint and bravery in an attempt to calm down Theodore, even after being shot. Even though Muniz was forced to shoot Theodore, he only did so after Johnson raised his gun to shoot again.

Ultimately, Theodore Johnson died by 'suicide-by-cop', and Muniz did what he had to do to end the confrontation. Sometimes, a police officer shooting down an opponent or assailant is the only way to do so.

****

What are some lessons that we can learn from the confrontation between David Muniz and Theodore Johnson?

Muniz did not want to have to shoot Theodore. It would have been instinctive to return fire as soon as Theodore shot, but Muniz went a step above this to stop and demand that Theodore lower his gun. Muniz truly did everything he could possibly do to end the situation peacefully, and he only opened fire when he had no choice.

Another important lesson we can learn from this is the importance of body camera footage. In this case, without the body camera footage, no one may have realized that Muniz acted as heroically as he did.

But at the same time, some claim that body camera technology can end up having the opposite effect on law enforcement officers.

Police departments and the officers who serve in them are regularly subjected to intense scrutiny by politicians and the general public. The whole point of using body camera technology is to document incidents that police officers find themselves in, so that cases of both true heroism (like in Muniz's case) or unnecessary brutality can be properly documented with clear proof of what happened.

Footage can also be used to prove that heroism was what happened when brutality is suspected, as was clearly what happened with Muniz.

But for other officers who find themselves in similar violent confrontations, even with the aid of body camera footage, what happened may not be clear due to a variety of other circumstances. For example, not everything that occurs in a violent incident involving police may end up getting caught on camera.

These officers who may be forced to act violently against an assailant may elect not to do so because they don't want acts of violence involving them to be caught on camera and serve as 'proof' of their brutality.

That's why some politicians and people have argued that body camera technology only serves to get in the way of law enforcement officers doing their job. Meanwhile, others contend that using footage is necessary to clearly differentiate between acts of heroism and brutality. Officer Muniz may not have received the recognition and acknowledgment for his heroic actions that he did if he had not been equipped with a body camera at the time.

Ultimately, it can go either way. Only you can decide for yourself if you think police officers wearing body cameras are an impediment or an important aid, but regardless, it's clear that David Muniz was a hero on that fateful day in March in Cleveland.

CHAPTER TWO

RAJKAMAL MEENA

What is the job of a police officer?

Think about that question for a bit.

Regardless of how you answer specifically, most people (in general) would probably answer that the job of a police officer involves helping ensure that members of the public are kept safe.

As we discussed before, much of the daily duties of a police officer involve what we would consider 'boring' tasks, such as paperwork or desk work.

But every once in a while, an extraordinary situation will arise where a police officer at the scene of an incident will be forced to rise above and beyond the call of duty. In other words, the daily tasks of a police officer may be rather uneventful and 'boring' in comparison to what we see in movies and TV, but every officer working needs to be prepared to act with extreme courage, bravery, and decisiveness should the situation demand it.

Police officers do not get to choose when these situations occur, so they need to ensure that they are always prepared to act decisively. Failing to do so could put someone's life at risk..., and one of the main jobs of a police officer is to ensure the safety of people and protect the lives of members of the general public.

And while some of these situations may involve police officers having to draw their weapons to physically confront those who are endangering members of the public, in other situations, there is no criminal or violent individual involved.

Let's talk about what happened to Indian Police Constable Rajkamal Meena in 2019 as an example.

****

Meena hadn't swum for over eight years. Little did he know that the next time he took to the water would be to save a 12-year-old boy from drowning.

Bawana is (by Indian standards) a small town in the Khayala locality in Delhi state in Northern India. With a population of around 23,000 people, the town is served by the Khayala police station.

Rajkamal Meena was one of the constables working at the Khayala station. A constable is the lowest police rank in India, and the daily tasks of most constables in India involve conducting patrol duties, serving eviction notices, engaging with members of the community, providing an active presence on the streets to reassure the public and deter crime, and searching for suspects.

One Tuesday afternoon in February 2019, Meena and two other police constables from the Khayala station were out looking for a suspect on the streets. They were preparing for a raid on a local building where they believed the suspect could be hiding.

At the same time, a local boy was out with two friends looking for coins and other metallic pieces that may have fallen into one of the local canals. The prior day, there had been a puja ceremony (a worship ritual), and it was not uncommon for coins or other valuables to be left behind.

The current of the canal was strong, but the boy and his friends tried to remain safe by searching on the outer banks of the water.

Meena was speaking with his two other constables nearby when he glanced over to the canal and noticed the boys playing and searching by the waters.

Meena was fully aware that the current in that area of the canal was very strong and that it was unsafe for children, or anyone for that matter, to be playing in. Less than a year before, two local engineering students had been sitting on the banks of the canal in the same location when one of them slipped into the water. The other student jumped into the water in an attempt to save his friend, but the current was too strong, and both ended up drowning.

Meena considered walking over to warn the boys to stop playing in the water, but he decided against it since he needed to remain focused on the preparations for the raid. Nonetheless, he continued to glance back at the boys every so often.

Unfortunately, the boy ended up creeping too far into the water and slipped and fell into the deeper part of the canal. Thrashing to the surface of the water, he tried to swim back to the shoreline, but the current was too strong and swept him away downstream.

His friends cried out for help and reached out with sticks in an attempt to get him back but to no avail. The boy was being carried rapidly downstream and was thrashing about, desperately trying to stay afloat.

Meena heard the cries of the boy and his friends and acted instantly without even thinking. He ran over to the banks of the canal and removed his jacket and shoes. He then plunged directly into the water. The fact that he hadn't gone swimming in over eight years didn't even cross his mind.

"The water was very cold," Meena later reported. "The last time I swam was in my village in Rajasthan, where every boy was taught to swim. I reached out to the boy and took him out."

When Meena dragged the boy back onto the shoreline, he appeared lifeless. Meena started thumping his chest, and in a matter of seconds, the boy regained consciousness and began coughing up water.

Locals began gathering around, and they provided jackets and towels to wrap Meena and the boy in, as both were shivering excessively from the coldness of the water.

Both were alive and okay, and that's what mattered. Meena and the boy were transferred to a hospital, where they were diagnosed with an infection and became very ill. But both made a recovery and in a matter of days, Meena was back on the force and the boy was back to playing with his friends…, albeit thankfully not by that area of the canal.

****

Meena did two things right. The first was that even though he was preparing for a raid with his other constables, he took notice of the boys playing by the water and was situationally aware of them.

A police officer must always have the safety of the public in mind first and foremost, and sometimes, this requires the police officer to be aware of multiple things happening at once. In this case, Meena had to focus on the preparations for the raid while also being keenly aware of the boys he noticed playing by the dangerous area of the canal, in which people had been known to drown.

If Meena had not been paying attention to the boys by the water, he would likely have been delayed by several seconds in running out to rescue the boy who had fallen in.

When Meena did drag the boy back up to the shoreline, he was completely unconscious, and it was only Meena's knowledge and application of CPR that saved his life and revived him. Had just a few more seconds passed by, it's not entirely positive that Meena's application of CPR would have worked - it may have been too late.

The second major thing that Meena did right is that he acted very quickly and without hesitating. Meena knew that he had not gone swimming in years, but he didn't allow that thought to make him hesitate for even a second. He ran over as soon as he heard the cries of the boys, removed his shoes and jacket so he could swim better, and jumped right into the frigid waters.

Meena could have drowned when he jumped in to save the boy, just like the engineering student who had also drowned trying to save his friend. But without thought, Meena put his own life in harm's way to save someone else, and thankfully, he was successful.

Later, Meena would say, "It is not just my duty as a civil servant, but also my dharma as a human being, to help others in need, and I did just that."

CHAPTER THREE

MARIO GUTIERREZ

If there's a common theme that we've been establishing in this book thus far, it's that while a cop's day-to-day life may be mundane and routine, they must always be ready on a moment's notice to put their life on the line to save an innocent.

Every one of the police officers whose incredible stories we're describing in this book didn't know they'd be getting involved in the situations that they did until mere minutes before they occurred.

This is one of the unpredictability factors of serving as a law enforcement officer in any department or any country. A police officer's every day is 'normal'...and then, out of nowhere, they'll either be dispatched to or randomly encounter a situation that requires them to spring into action and put their life on the line.

What makes things more harrowing are the opponents against which police officers often find themselves. In this true story, you're about to read, a police officer unexpectedly found himself facing a crazed arsonist who attempted to set fire to a gas station..., and this arsonist was also exceptionally skilled with a knife in close-quarters combat!

****

Fifty-five-year-old Miami-Dade Police Officer Mario Gutierrez was just five years away from retirement. He had been serving Miami-Dade as a law enforcement officer for 21 years, and seven of those years were spent as a motorcycle officer.

It was October 2013, and the day was an unusually slow one for Gutierrez. He was near Miami International Airport patrolling an intersection. The area surrounding the airport is among the busiest with traffic in the entire city of Miami, but today, it was even more so.

Gutierrez glanced around while patrolling the intersection. Suddenly, he noticed clouds of smoke coming from the ground. A Shell gas station sign was visible near the smoke, so Gutierrez's first thought was that the gas station was on fire.

As he raced over to the Shell station, it didn't take long for Gutierrez to realize that he was right. A gas hose was stretched out over the property of the gas station, and an arsonist was attempting to set two 8,000-gallon underground fuel tanks on fire.

"When I saw that, I panicked, because I realized what was going to happen," Gutierrez later recalled. "And it scared me because I thought, 'Wow, we are going to die. This is going to be a catastrophe.'"

The first thing Gutierrez did was activate the emergency shut-off valve to the fuel pumps. This would, hopefully, remove the threat of the fuel pumps catching on fire and exploding, which would have caused damage on a catastrophic level.

Then he turned his attention to the arsonist.

The arsonist was 51-year-old Dominique Jean, who was also armed with a screwdriver and an eight-inch blade knife.

Gutierrez then approached Jean intending to arrest him. He drew his taser from his duty belt, thinking that he would incapacitate Jean with the taser before cuffing him.

But Jean had no intention of being handcuffed and taken into custody. Rather, he resolved to fight Gutierrez tooth and nail.

Drawing the eight-inch knife and the screwdriver, Jean lunged forward toward Gutierrez and tackled him to the ground. Waving the knife about in a frenzy, he slashed the knife across Gutierrez's chest!

****

"I have to stay alive for my family," was Gutierrez's first thought as the serrated edge of the long knife sliced from one side of his chest to the other and inflicted severe pain that shot all over his body.

But the moment Jean had slashed the knife across Gutierrez was the moment he sealed his fate that day.

"When he stabbed me and I thought of my family, I became the predator, and he became the prey, and that's why I survived," Gutierrez said afterwards, "that is what saved my life: my training and my determination to survive."

The two men grappled together on the pavement of the gas station, with Jean on top and slashing his knife repeatedly across Gutierrez. Gutierrez raised his arms in an attempt to deflect the blows, resulting in long slashes hacking his arms, wrists, and hands.

Gutierrez attempted to draw his duty pistol, holstered at this side, but when he managed to draw it out, Jean bit Gutierrez's thumb while continuing to stab and slash him repeatedly.

Jean managed to wrestle his hand free and fired five shots at point-blank range in rapid succession. All five of the bullets struck Jean, and after a moment, he rolled off Gutierrez in a growing pool of blood from both of the men.

The battle between Gutierrez and Jean lasted a total of 20 seconds, during which Gutierrez had fired a total of five shots and Jean had slashed or stabbed Gutierrez with the knife no less than 12 times.

"All I thought about was he's not going to kill me," Gutierrez said, "I'm going to win because I want to see my family."

Dominique Jean later died at the scene.

****

Miami Police Officers Chris Garcia and Juan Leon were in their patrol vehicle around three blocks away when they received the call for help.

Twenty seconds later, they were at the Shell gas station. Gutierrez was on his knees and bleeding profusely from all over his body, while Jean's lifeless body was lying motionless, with the knife still in his hand.

Garcia and Leon wasted no time.

"I knew he was in trouble," Leon recalled. "His brown shirt was completely covered. It was red. It wasn't brown, it was red. I knew he had to get to the hospital right away."

Seconds later, Gutierrez was put into the patrol car thanks to the efforts of Leon and Garcia, and they were soon racing to the nearest hospital. Believing he was near death, Gutierrez related what had happened to the two officers so his account would be known.

Gutierrez nearly fainted several times en route to the hospital. Leon and Garcia knew that Gutierrez passing out perhaps would be fatal given the amount of blood he had lost and was continuing to lose. Each time they noticed Gutierrez beginning to faint, they yelled in his face to keep him awake.

Their combined efforts succeeded. They arrived at the hospital, and nurses loaded Gutierrez onto a wheeled stretcher to take him inside and tend to his wounds.

****

Gutierrez had multiple surgeries while at the hospital, but he made a full recovery.

For a while, Gutierrez felt guilty that he had failed to do his job. He believed that he should have detected Jean's presence earlier and that he had let him under his guard.

But Gutierrez's fellow police officers reassured him that he was a hero and had succeeded in stopping Jean before he could have caused far worse damage.

Had Gutierrez arrived just a few seconds later at the gas station, Jean likely would have succeeded in his objective of setting fire to the fuel tanks. The resulting explosion would have not only destroyed the gas station and inflicted much damage on the immediate vicinity, but it also may have caused the deaths of dozens if not hundreds of people as well.

This was Jean's goal, but he was stopped by Gutierrez. And even though Jean had the upper hand at first and managed to inflict several deep knife wounds into Gutierrez's body, he realized too late that he was up against a man who was a fighter.

Gutierrez took over a dozen knife stabbings and slashings but still managed to take out his handgun to finish the fight. An officer who reacted slower or who didn't have Gutierrez's willpower may have been overwhelmed by Jean's vicious attack, but Gutierrez was a warrior at heart, and his combat skills eclipsed Jean's.

****

It had always been Gutierrez's dream to become a police officer. He had been working as a washing machine repairman for over 12 years. He had applied repeatedly to the Miami Police Department to become a law enforcement officer, but his applications were always denied, either because of a hiring freeze or because other applications were selected.

But Gutierrez refused to give up. He had the heart of a warrior, and he knew he was destined to serve with the Miami Police Department. So, he kept on submitting his applications anyway.

One day, after many years, Gutierrez checked his mailbox and was astonished to see that his latest application had been selected.

"When that letter came, it was like winning the lottery," Gutierrez said.

Think about it this way: if Gutierrez had given up submitting his application to the Miami Police Department after many failures, he could not have been there that day to confront Jean. And while another officer may have been there instead, their bravery, skill, and willpower may not have been at the same level as Gutierrez's.

Receiving multiple knife wounds is no easy thing. Just one slash or stabbing alone can cause you to go into an instant state of shock that delays your reaction time. Multiple wounds will also result in more blood loss, reducing your ability to fight back.

Making matters worse, Gutierrez was on blood thinners at the time and was especially susceptible to fainting from a loss of blood.

But Gutierrez refused to give up, and his desire to be reunited with his family (his first thought when Jean's blade first slashed across his chest) allowed him to keep on fighting.

After his retirement, Gutierrez returned to a quiet life of working on firearms as a gunsmith and on cars. But he still misses being in uniform and working with his fellow brothers and sisters in arms.

"Police officers are everyday people that live in the community that decides to take on the burden, the responsibility, of deterring the predators that are out preying on society," Gutierrez reminds us, "some of them lose their lives."

The entire fight between Gutierrez and Jean was captured on camera. Watching the footage after, Gutierrez insisted that he couldn't remember 80% of what went down.

"It was a very vicious fight," he recalled. "It happened very fast. The speed was very fast. To break it down like that was unbelievable. It was just a stressful night and it was pretty hard for me to go through it but I did it."

Gutierrez's wife, Laura, shared the belief that her husband's warrior mindset kept him alive and brought him back home.

"He was very well trained," she said, "he had the right mindset. He always said I will fight and stay alive and do whatever I have to do to protect this community and other lives and will always come home for you."

****

Following his recovery in 2013, Gutierrez received the Medal of Valor (the nation's highest honor for members of law enforcement) from President Barack Obama as well as the Congressional Badge of Bravery. He was declared the Miami-Dade Benevolent Association Officer of the Year in 2013 as well.

"I'm not a special man," Gutierrez insisted after receiving the Medal of Valor award. "I'm just a regular guy doing his job."

CHAPTER FOUR

MICHAEL GREGOREK

It's not just people who sometimes need saving from police officers. Our furry companions sometimes need saving too.

An event that occurred in early February 2022 in Douglas County, Colorado was a stark reminder of that fact.

A Douglas County Sheriff deputy named Michael Gregorek was responding to a call of a vehicle that was on fire. He received the call around 4:30 p.m. About a month earlier, he'd received another call regarding a suspect who had been throwing Molotov cocktails at vehicles.

Arriving at the scene, Gregorek indeed saw a burning vehicle engulfed in flames…, and a man who was throwing objects right at it.

His heart racing, Gregorek realized that he was dealing with the same Molotov cocktail suspect he had been called about before.

Bringing his car to a rapid stop, Gregorek exited the vehicle with his hand over his duty weapon.

"My dog's in the car!" The suspect yelled to Gregorek. "My dog's in the car! My dog's in the car."

It took a matter of seconds for Gregorek to comprehend that the 'suspect' was not throwing Molotov cocktails at the car at all. Instead, he was throwing items at the windows of the car in an attempt to break them!

"My dog is in the car; my dog is in the car!" the 'suspect' continued to yell at Gregorek.

It was then that Gregorek heard, over the roar of the flames, barking from inside the car.

And then Gregorek realized that this man was not the Molotov cocktail suspect at all.

Gregorek withdrew his retractable baton from his belt and then rushed over to the rear of the burning vehicle. With one hit, he smashed the window open.

The dog inside was still barking but too scared and confused to jump out himself. The owner of the dog then raced over and attempted to climb in to pull the dog out, but the smoke was too thick, and he was forced to step aside.

Gregorek then climbed into the vehicle himself and grabbed the barking animal before hoisting him out to safety.

"Hank!" The owner cried, referring to the dog as he reunited with him.

To ensure that Hank was completely free of any flames, Gregorek picked him up and ran him over to the snow. When the firefighters arrived on the scene, Gregorek was able to inform them with confidence that Hank was not alight.

A man who lived in a nearby neighborhood witnessed the incident and arrived on the scene to give Gregorek a drink of water. By sheer luck, the man's wife was a veterinarian, and he said she could take a look at Hank to make sure he was okay.

She checked him out and confirmed that Hank was in good health.

****

An investigation of the incident later revealed what had happened. Hank's owner had parked his vehicle next to a building and left Hank in the vehicle with the window halfway open for air.

The fire was most likely caused by an electrical disturbance under the console or dashboard of the vehicle and was accidental.

The incident, caught on camera, found its way onto the internet after being released to the media. It became an online sensation as people all over the world lauded Gregorek for his bravery and decisiveness.

"Once I arrived on the scene, the very first thing I saw was a gentleman who ended up being the owner of the vehicle, and the owner of the dog, throwing something at the back of the vehicle," Gregorek recalled.

Gregorek acted quickly and became a rescuer when he heard the dog's owner shout repeatedly, "my dog is in the car!"

"It flipped the switch from 'It's obviously not a crime' to 'Now we have a life,'" said Gregorek, who himself is a dog owner.

Gregorek climbing into the back of the blazing car was also necessary to save Hank's life. Gregorek could see Hank inside the car after breaking the window open, but he could also see that Hank was frozen up from distress and wouldn't be getting out on his own. That was when Gregorek realized that he would have to climb in himself if Hank were to have any chance of survival.

****

There were several things that Gregorek did right to save Hank's life. The first is that Gregorek recalled the Molotov cocktail suspect from a month prior. And when he arrived on the scene and saw the dog's owner hurling things at the car, he felt his suspicions were confirmed.

But the moment Gregorek heard, "my dog is in the car, my dog is in the car!" repeatedly, he also wasted no time in switching mental gears to take action and rescue the trapped animal inside. This shows quick thinking and decisiveness on Gregorek's part, which are critical aspects that need to be practiced by anyone serving in law enforcement.

This was also good communication on the dog owner's part. Had he not been clear about what the problem was or stayed silent, Gregorek would likely have continued to consider him as the Molotov cocktail suspect. In this case, seconds would have gone by, at which point it may have been too late to save Hank.

This shows how important it is for civilians and law enforcement officers alike to properly communicate with one another, especially in times of crisis where seconds count massively.

To this day, Gregorek continues to visit Hank from time to time. Even though Hank still lives with his owner, he and Gregorek formed a strong bond that day that is likely to last for the rest of their lives.

"I would've done the same thing whether it be a baby, a human, a dog, or a cat," Gregorek reported after the event. "A life is a life. You kind of treat it as such in a situation like that."

CHAPTER FIVE

DONALD THOMPSON

Dogs are not the only ones who sometimes need to be rescued from burning cars. That's because, more often than not, it's people rather than animals who find themselves trapped in vehicles that have been set ablaze.

On Christmas Day 2013, LAPD Officer Donald Thompson found that out for himself.

Even though it was Christmas, it was actually an ordinary workday for both Thompson and his wife. But perhaps that was a good thing because if it hadn't been, it's unlikely that Thompson would have found himself in the situation that he did…, and the people he ended up saving may not have been saved.

Thompson was an active-duty officer and his wife worked as the manager at a restaurant, which is why they both had to work on Christmas. So, Thompson dropped their daughter off at a friend's house and then headed in to report for duty. Thompson opted to get to work ahead of his actual shift, so his coworkers could leave early for Christmas.

Thompson was driving to work southbound on the 405 Freeway and, since it was Christmas Day, the traffic was very minimal.

It was then that Thompson witnessed a Mercedes-Benz station wagon heading northbound suddenly crash into the center divider of the road. The moment the vehicle hit the median, it burst into flames. With the light traffic, the event was instantly noticeable.

"After it hit, a huge ball of fire happened," Thompson later recalled.

Thompson pulled off to the side of the road and hit the brakes of his police cruiser to bring it to a screeching halt.

He then exited his vehicle and ran over to the blazing Mercedes, jumping over two barricades in the process.

The driver's door to the Mercedes was badly damaged, but it wasn't open. Thompson had to put his hands on the extremely hot surface of the door to pry it open.

The entire Mercedes had been set ablaze, but Thompson acted as if the fire was no issue. He ran straight up to the driver's side of the vehicle, drew his knife, and reached a part of his body into the car to cut the seatbelt free. The driver was not moving and was slumped over, so Thompson ascertained he was unconscious.

Thompson could feel the intense heat from the fire, but he ignored it and continued to do his work by cutting the seatbelt.

"You feel like you're in a rotisserie," Thompson said when he recollected the event later. "I noted how much heat I was experiencing. I could feel the heat on all my exposed skin."

Dealing with the combination of the intense flames licking away at his skin and the smoke bearing down into his lungs was among the hardest challenges Thompson had ever dealt with in his life, but he tried hard to stay focused on getting the unconscious man out of the car.

"What you instinctively want to do is turn around and just run away," said Thompson. "You've got pain, and there's all this heat. Now there's smoke. I just had to bear down. One of the hardest things I've had to do was stay focused and not just back away and turn around and run."

Suddenly, the fire grew larger, and a flame licked up to engulf Thompson's entire arm. He instinctively drew back and yelled in pain, patting his arm down with his other hand to get the flames out. Then, without even thinking about it, he reached back into the car again.

Finally, Thompson managed to get the seatbelt free. The unconscious man slumped forward again, and Thompson grabbed a hold of him with both arms to withdraw him out of the car.

Bystanders were running over to Thompson by this point, and they helped him to pull the man completely out of the car and away from the flames.

****

"He's my miracle worker," Bill McWhorter said after the incident.

McWhorter was the man trapped inside of the car. He was a 72-year-old architectural and landscape designer who blacked out while driving due to a medical emergency. This is what caused the Mercedes that he was driving to spin out of control and crash into the center divider on the highway.

"I wouldn't be here today if it weren't for Donald Thompson," McWhorter later said. "Not everyone would do that. Had he not come along, I wouldn't have made it, I'm sure."

As it turned out, Thompson having to work on Christmas had been a good thing. Had it not been for Thompson, McWhorter surely would have died a slow and horrific death in that Mercedes before anyone arrived.

Amazingly, McWhorter's injuries sustained from the crash and fire were minimal. He only suffered a few cracked ribs and some minor burns.

Thompson's injuries, on the other hand, were far more severe and substantial. He suffered numerous first- and second-degree burns all over his arms and torso.

The Los Angeles Police Commission later assigned Thompson the Department's Medal of Valor, based on the recommendation of the Chief of Police Charles Beck, who served as the department's chief from 2009 to 2018.

"Thompson went above and beyond the call of duty in his efforts to remove the unconscious accident victim and save his life," Beck wrote in a memo detailing his recommendation.

Thompson himself said that his motivation to save McWhorter's life was the only motivation he needed to take the actions that he did. Even though Thompson didn't personally know McWhorter, it didn't matter. He knew that McWhorter was loved by other people, and Thompson thought, "What if someone I loved was trapped in that car?"

"Imagine if it was maybe your husband or your child, mother or father," said Thompson. "That person there was someone's loved one. No plaque, citation or acknowledgment could take the place of someone looking you in the eye and saying, 'Thank you for saving my life.'"

The first-degree burns and severe smoke inhalation in his lungs that Thompson suffered to get McWhorter out of the car were horrific, and these are injuries that he will have to live with for the rest of his life. A person of lesser bravery than Thompson surely would have recoiled from the car at the first instance of being burned, but Thompson managed to persevere to rescue McWhorter.

Officers who have the courage and fortitude to do as Thompson did are the exact kinds of police officers that we need more of today.

In 2016, Donald Thompson was awarded the Medal of Valor by President Barack Obama, the same award that had been bestowed upon Mario Gutierrez.

CHAPTER SIX

TERRANCE YEAKEY

In April 1995, the United States suffered one of its worst terrorist attacks of the pre-9/11 era.

A bomb went off in the Alfred P. Murrah Federal Building in Oklahoma City. The explosion resulted in the deaths of 168 people and the injuries of over 680. Among the dead were over 19 children, who perished in the daycare center that was in the vicinity of the explosion.

To this day, the Oklahoma City Bombing remains the deadliest domestic terrorist act in the United States, and it's the second deadliest terrorist attack on U.S. soil overall, after the 9/11 attacks.

The Oklahoma City Bombing was a horrific event that will never be forgotten. But what might be forgotten, if we fail to tell and retell their stories, are the heroic acts of the law enforcement officers serving in Oklahoma City who responded to the bombing that day. The lives of many people trapped in the rubble and collapsed buildings were saved by police officers and other emergency responders who wasted no time in racing to the aftermath and getting to work.

The name of one of those officers was Terrance Yeakey. Yeakey would save the lives of four people that day. But just over a year after the bombings, Yeakey himself would tragically be found dead under the most mysterious circumstances. Even though Yeakey's death was officially ruled as a suicide, most people who knew him refused to accept that Yeakey had truly killed himself.

We'll talk about Yeakey's heroic actions, the specifics surrounding his tragic death, and why he deserves to be remembered. But to understand this story in its proper context, we first need to understand the Oklahoma City Bombing and what exactly happened.

****

The Oklahoma City Bombing was perpetrated by two anti-government extremists, Terry Nichols and Timothy McVeigh. The explosion occurred just after 9:00 a.m. on

April 19, 1995, and it destroyed over one-third of the Alfred P. Murrah Federal Building complex while also damaging over 300 other buildings and destroying over 86 cars within a 16-block radius.

Most tragic of all was the fact that 168 people were killed and over 680 were injured. Immediately following the bombing, emergency response teams got to work to recover people who were trapped in the rubble and to apprehend the perpetrators.

McVeigh was discovered 90 minutes later when he was stopped by an Oklahoma City Patrolman for driving a vehicle without a license plate and possession of illegal weapons. Nichols was then linked to the attack after a forensic investigation. Both were charged with the crime within days.

Five years later, in 2000, the Oklahoma City National Memorial was constructed and erected on the site where the Murrah Federal Building once stood. Each year, remembrance services are held yearly on April 19 at 9:02 a.m., the time of the explosion.

Because of the sheer magnitude of the incident, the Oklahoma City Bombing will never be forgotten, and neither will the names of the perpetrators.

But what has been largely forgotten since the bombing are the names of the police officers and emergency first responders who came to the aid of those trapped in the rubble and got to work saving lives! The death count may have been very high that day, but it would have been higher had it not been for the efforts of those who responded.

Let's talk about the stories of one of those who responded on that day.

****

Oklahoma City Police Officer Terrance Yeakey was the first police officer at the site of the bombing.

Yeakey was 29 years old at the time of the bombing. After his high school years, he joined the United States military and for a time was stationed in Saudi Arabia. After his time in the military, Yeakey decided to embark on a career in law enforcement. He officially joined the Oklahoma City Police Department in 1989.

Despite his youth, Yeakey was well-liked and respected by his friends and colleagues. He had been serving with the Oklahoma City Police Department (OCPD) for six years by the time of the bombing, and he had proven himself to be both very effective at his job and very pleasant to be around.

Another reason why Yeakey was so well-liked by his colleagues was because of his big heart, good intentions, and personable nature. His fellow officers after the bombing described Yeakey as someone who "brought joy to the department" and served as an inspiration to the other officers on the force, including his elders.

Yeakey was also one of the officers who taught the OCPD's DARE (Department Youth Anti-Drug Program), where he worked with students one-on-one to overcome or avoid drug addictions. The students, who Yeakey worked with likewise, described him as a very positive force in their lives and the Oklahoma community as a whole. When his death happened a year later, letters from these children poured into the media by the dozens, praising Yeakey for his efforts and his thoughtfulness in working with them.

After his death, people would remember Yeakey for his loud voice, funny sense of humor, and seemingly effortless ability to switch between being firm and imposing as a cop while humble and likable as an ordinary man in his personal life.

Had Yeakey not been at the site of the bombing, it's very possible that he would still be with us today, continuing with his good work. There were many grave tragedies when that bomb went off, and the death of Yeakey in the aftermath was one of them. His efforts saved the lives of several people trapped in the rubble.

****

When the bombing occurred on that fateful day in 1995, Yeakey and his friend and colleague Officer Jim Ramsey were dispatched to the Alfred P. Murrah building where the explosion had occurred.

As soon as they pulled up to the building, Yeakey wasted no time. He raced out of his vehicle and into the burning rubble - he could hear the screams of people trapped inside.

For several hours, Yeakey worked his way through the rubble and up and down multiple layers of the building in an effort to locate trapped and wounded survivors inside. Even though the building was in imminent danger of total collapse - which surely would have caused the death of anyone inside - Yeakey acted with no concern for his own life, only for the lives of others in the building.

One by one, Yeakey found wounded people trapped in the building, lifted them up, and carried them to ambulances that were gathering outside. Each time he dropped off a person in an ambulance, he immediately ran back into the building to find and rescue somebody else.

After rescuing multiple people, Yeakey fell through two floors of the building, landing on and gravely injuring his back.

The exact number of people that Yeakey pulled out of the rubble that day remains in dispute, with most estimates ranging from three to five or more.

Regardless of the exact number of people he saved, there's simply no question that Terrance Yeakey was one of the heroes of the aftermath of the Oklahoma City Bombing. It's certainly because of his efforts and the efforts of other emergency responders like him that the death count from the bombing was not higher than it was. Yet their names are not remembered like McVeigh's or Nichols'.

Yeakey surely would have gone on to serve a complete and fruitful career in law enforcement, but to the horror of the department and other members of the Oklahoma City community, his life would be cut short abruptly only a year later.

****

Terrance Yeakey never wanted to be a hero. Members of the OCPD remember him as a reluctant hero whose main concern was saving lives and who didn't like the hero-status he acquired in the news media in the aftermath of the bombing.

"There are some people that like to be heroes and some that don't; he was not one that wanted that," Yeakey's supervisor Lieutenant Joe Ann Randall would later say.

Yeakey was a very humble man who had dedicated his life to a career that was focused on saving the lives of other people, whether that was hauling people out of the rubble from the bombing or stopping teens from a life of drug abuse as part of his service with the DARE program.

The department recognized Yeakey's achievements, and he was scheduled to receive the OCPD's Medal of Valor on May 11, 1996. It was not an award that Yeakey asked for because of his humility, but it was one that he was willing to accept.

Then another tragedy struck.

On May 8, 1996, just three days before Yeakey was to publicly receive the Medal of Valor, he was found dead near El Reno, his hometown around a half hour's drive from Oklahoma City.

Yeakey was found with knife cuts on his wrists, arms, and his neck…, and a gunshot wound in his head. The authorities ruled his death a suicide. The official narrative was that Yeakey had committed suicide by slitting his wrists and neck and then shooting himself in the head with a handgun.

The death of Yeakey served as a deep shock to his family, friends, colleagues at the OCPD, and the members of the Oklahoma City community. He had left no note, and no one who knew or interacted with him recalled any suspicious behavior in the days preceding his death.

Officer Jim Ramsey, who had responded to the bombing with Yeakey, believed that he had committed suicide because of his guilt over failing to rescue more people from the bombing. When Yeakey fell from those two stories and badly injured his back, it incapacitated him from rescuing more people.

Some other people were still alive at the time that Yeakey fell inside the building, but they later died. Yeakey had expressed to Ramsey that he believed he could have saved them.

Also, while Yeakey was very successful in his career as a law enforcement officer, his family life was difficult. He and his wife had divorced, and she had even barred him from seeing his two young daughters. Ramsey speculated that Yeakey's guilt over failing to rescue more people combined with not seeing his daughters was just too much for him to handle.

Nonetheless, there were and are many people who heavily dispute the official narrative of Yeakey's death. While it is true that Yeakey did express guilt to multiple colleagues and friends for failing to rescue more people from the bombing, most of those people later said that they didn't believe this guilt would lead a man of Yeakey's character and virtue to have suicidal thoughts.

That's because even though Yeakey was guilt-ridden, he also knew that he had an entire career ahead of him. He could spend decades saving or helping more lives. Surely, this knowledge would have outweighed the guilt that Yeakey felt over his own-perceived shortcomings in the bombings?

Furthermore, while it is true that Yeakey was experiencing difficulties with his homelife, this was beginning to turn around. Yeakey and his ex-wife were on the path to reconciling before his death and were even discussing a remarriage. Yeakey's ex-wife herself said that she does not believe Yeakey committed suicide.

So, if Yeakey didn't commit suicide, the question becomes who killed him, and why?

To date, the official cause of death of Yeakey is suicide. There are many conspiracy theories over why the Alfred P. Murrah Federal Building was bombed that fateful day, and the idea that Yeakey was murdered rather than committed suicide is one of those theories.

For instance, some claim that Yeakey knew more about why the bombings occurred than he was willing to publicly disclose, at least at the time. Some people who knew Yeakey stated that he was spending a lot of his time investigating the circumstances of the bombing. Some said that his work performance had even suffered because of how much time and effort he was putting into his own investigation - and that he was getting close to putting all the pieces together about what had happened.

The truth surrounding the Oklahoma City Bombing and the death of Terrance Yeakey may never be solved, and for now, much of what happened remains a major mystery.

But even though this aspect of Yeakey may be a mystery for now, the fact that he was a true hero both during the bombing and in his career as a law enforcement officer is not a mystery at all.

It's incredibly important that we remember Terrance Yeakey, along with the other heroic police officers who have lost their lives in the line of duty.

Serving as a police officer means your life is always on the line in the interest of protecting or saving other members of the public. Police officers like Yeakey represent the finest examples of the people serving in uniform who we can all look up to, and whose courage and bravery we could aspire to emulate in our own lives.

CHAPTER SEVEN

JESSE HARTNETT

In January 2016, a seemingly random and yet deadly incident took place that sent shockwaves throughout the United States and the law enforcement community.

In the streets of Philadelphia, a man named Edward Archer walked right up to the patrol car of Officer Jesse Hartnett, inserted a Glock 9mm pistol through the window, and shot Hartnett multiple times at point-blank range.

Reading that, you may think that Hartnett died right then and there..., but he didn't. Even though perhaps most people, including most law enforcement officers, would have been unable to react immediately after being shot multiple times at close range, Hartnett acted as if he hadn't been shot at all.

Instead, as Archer took off running in his attempted hit-and-run, Hartnett actually got out of his patrol vehicle and chased after Archer!

****

Jesse James Hartnett was 33 years old and a four-year veteran of the Philadelphia Police Department.

Hartnett had made it his life's mission to serve his country and protect innocent lives. A graduate of Monsignor Bonner High School in 2001, Hartnett enlisted in the United States Coast Guard after the 9/11 attacks occurred.

Hartnett would serve with the Coast Guard on active duty until 2008, before switching to the Coast Guard Reserve in 2009. While a part of the Coast Guard Reserve, Hartnett became a police officer for the East Lansdowne Police Force before transferring to the Philadelphia Police Department in 2011.

He had been serving there for four years and had just exited the Coast Guard Reserve at the time of the shooting.

The day of that fateful shooting was as routine as any other. That's part of serving as a police officer: most working days are routinely normal, and when major incidents occur that require the police officers to spring into action and put their lives on the line, it's often when they least expect it.

****

Edward Archer was 30 years old, unemployed, and living with his mother when the shooting took place. His mother lived in Yeadon, a small town about 20 minutes outside of Philadelphia.

Archer took a distinctively different path in life than Hartnett did. In his teenage years, those who knew him said that Archer took an intense interest in Islam. This interest in Islam turned into commitment and then a conversion when Archer became an adult.

He adopted the Muslim name Abdul Shaheed and made the pilgrimage to Mecca in 2011. He then traveled to and studied Islam in Egypt for over six months in 2012. During this time, he also learned Arabic.

During his time in Egypt, Archer claimed that he was the subject of racist comments from those living in the area. As a result of this, he cut his time in Egypt short and returned to Philadelphia, where he began to get further involved in the local Islamic community.

After the shooting, a law enforcement investigation found that Archer's trip to Egypt was primarily paid for by a group of Muslim men living in Philadelphia. Since Archer was unemployed, he could not have afforded the trip himself, but it is common practice in Islamic communities for local Muslims to give donations to newcomers to the religion to help finance such trips.

Archer was well known to those in the Philadelphia Islamic community. For instance, the Imam (the title given to one who leads Muslim worshippers in prayer) of the local Masjid Mujahideen Mosque, Asim Abdur Rashid, reported that Archer was very devout. He was also actively involved in the local Islamic community, and other Muslims living in Philadelphia reported the same thing.

In March 2015, Archer began getting into trouble with law enforcement. He pleaded guilty to incidents of aggravated assault, a firearm offense, and making terroristic threats. One of these incidents involved Archer and two associates confronting the husband of Archer's ex-wife. Even though he was sentenced to prison, Archer's sentence was reduced, and he was released and placed on probation.

Archer's mother told police after the shooting that he had sustained head injuries from playing football in his youth and also claimed that he had suffered from a mental illness. For example, she stated that Archer would repeatedly say that he could hear voices in his head. Those who knew Archer in high school said that he mostly kept to himself, but they claimed he was not religious. This indicates that Archer, at least publicly, had converted to Islam after his high school years.

After the incident, Archer confessed that he believed Allah had ordered him to commit the attack against Hartnett. Archer targeted a police officer specifically, he said - because they defended laws that violated what Allah taught in the Quran, the Islamic holy book.

****

On the night in question, Hartnett was in uniform and driving his Chevy Impala patrol car near midnight in West Philadelphia.

Archer, wearing a white thawb (a robe that is traditionally worn by Muslim men) and armed with a Glock 17 - 9mm pistol that held 17 rounds in the magazine, suddenly rushed the Impala and shoved his gun through the window on the driver's door.

In rapid succession, Archer fired 13 shots directly at Hartnett at point-blank range. On instinct, Hartnett immediately raised his left arm to absorb three of the bullets.

Amazingly, the other 10 rounds missed Hartnett.

Archer stopped shooting and turned to run away.

Despite being badly wounded and bleeding profusely from his shattered arm, Hartnett managed to bring the vehicle to a stop and exit it. He then took off running after Archer while drawing his duty sidearm.

Hartnett aimed and fired three shots at Archer, one of which struck Archer in the buttocks. Archer stumbled but continued running.

Hartnett temporarily stopped the chase and grabbed his radio to call in for help. Other police officers in the vicinity responded to Hartnett's call and continued the chase. The wounded Archer was found and apprehended around a block away from the site of the shooting.

It was later discovered that the Glock Archer used in the shooting was itself a police-issue handgun and had been stolen from the home of a police officer in 2013.

****

There's no denying that a miracle saved Hartnett that day. Archer had fired a total of 13 rounds directly at him, but 10 of those rounds somehow missed him. And the three rounds that did hit him struck him in the arm. Despite losing a lot of blood, Hartnett was able to receive prompt and successful medical attention following the shooting at Penn Presbyterian Hospital.

After his arrest, Archer told investigators, "I follow Allah. I pledge allegiance to the Islamic State, and that's why I did what I did."

Richard Ross, Philadelphia's Police Commissioner, said that Archer had indeed referenced the Islamic State under questioning; it was undetermined if the attack had any connection to ISIS or any other organization associated with terrorism.

Ross referred to the ambush as an assassination attempt. "Archer," he said, "just came out of nowhere and started firing at him [Hartnett] with one aim and one aim only, to kill him."

For his part, Hartnett was in a very serious but stable condition following the shooting. He remained in good spirits and underwent surgery to help repair his arm. The bullets that Archer had fired fractured his arm and also severed many nerves. Even though Hartnett sustained nerve damage and a massive loss of blood, he made a full recovery and continues to use his arm to this day.

****

Hartnett was saved that day for two reasons. The first, as we've discussed already, was a miracle, whether by sheer luck or an act of God. Ten of the 13 bullets fired at close range completely missed him; had just one of those bullets struck Hartnett in a vital region of his body, the outcome may indeed have been completely different.

But Hartnett was also saved because of his quick thinking and reaction to the situation. Most people who get shot in any region of their body, at close range or not, would likely be too shocked and astonished to do anything to react.

Hartnett hit the brakes of the car and got out of the vehicle to give chase to Archer. As a police officer, he knew it was his duty to apprehend criminals, and he knew that Archer posed a massive and immediate threat to other people nearby.

That's why despite being shot multiple times and bleeding profusely, Hartnett gave chase to Archer.

Hartnett simply refused to give up.

"It's both confounding and astonishing that he was able to escape it, and I can't say enough for his bravery and how he conducted himself," Ross said in recognition of what Hartnett did.

Another thing that Hartnett did right was to get in contact with other law enforcement officers to call them in. Hartnett knew that he was bleeding badly and that he could pass out at any moment. If that had happened, Archer would have had a good chance of escaping that night.

By calling in his fellow officers, Hartnett ensured that Archer had no chance of getting away with what he did.

****

The FBI assisted the Philadelphia Police Department in the investigation following the incident because terrorism was suspected. FBI agents searched two nearby residences that were connected to Archer, and they also began to look through his phone records and online activities.

Three days following the shooting, a woman who remains unidentified stopped a police officer patrolling the street and informed him that Archer was part of a radical group that also consisted of at least three other men. She also warned that Archer was "not the most radical out of the four" and that the threat to Philadelphia's law enforcement officers was not over.

She also warned that the other three members of these extremist groups were a frequent presence in the area where Hartnett was shot.

This tip meant that all law enforcement agencies in Philadelphia were put on high alert. To this end, all police officers were ordered to work in pairs rather than alone.

Six days after the shooting, the then-FBI Director announced that the Bureau would be investigating the shooting as a terrorist attack. A day later, Comey revealed that the investigation had not found any evidence that Archer was connected to terrorist groups, and no other planned attacks in Philadelphia or the surrounding region were uncovered.

Archer was arraigned and later, in February 2018, convicted of attempted murder and aggravated assault. He was sentenced to serve the maximum term that was available for the crime, which was between 48 and 97 years. He remains behind bars to this day.

****

Today, the attack on Jesse Hartnett by Edward Archer is commonly cited as an example of lone-wolf terrorism. The term refers to violent attacks perpetrated by individuals against members of the public. These individuals may have a radical ideology or set of beliefs to justify (in their mind) their violent actions but ultimately lack substantial overseas connections.

Unfortunately, lone-wolf attacks like this have been on the rise in the United States throughout the 21st century. The San Bernardino attack in 2015, for instance, is also cited as an example of this phenomenon, where individuals are inspired by violently radical ideologies but ultimately do not appear to have connections to terrorist organizations overseas.

It's because of the increasing prevalence of lone-wolf attacks that police officers have to be on a much higher alert in their day-to-day lives. They may be randomly targeted by mentally unstable individuals with radical ideologies and a willingness to commit violence - like Archer.

All police officers can look up to Jesse Hartnett as an example of how to respond to a lone-wolf attack. Despite being caught by surprise and grievously wounded, Hartnett stayed calm and reacted with decisiveness. He shielded his torso with his arm to absorb several of the bullets, chased Archer despite his injuries, and radioed in for help so other police officers in the area could converge on Archer.

Yes, it was a complete miracle that 10 of the 12 bullets missed Hartnett. But it's also clear that Hartnett demonstrated exactly how a police officer should react as the victim of a lone-wolf attack.

CHAPTER EIGHT

JAMES BEATON

Our next story takes us across the Atlantic to Britain and also a bit farther back in time: March 20, 1972.

It was 8:00 p.m. and a fancy Rolls-Royce limousine was driving down the London mall toward Buckingham Palace.

Suddenly, a white Ford Escort pulled out in front of the limo, bringing it to a screeching halt. The man inside the Escort was named Ian Ball and he was armed.

One of the women inside the limo was Princess Anne - and Ball was there to kidnap her!

****

The limo was being driven by Alex Callender, one of the royal chauffeurs serving Buckingham Palace. Metropolitan Police Inspector James Beaton was in the car with him.

68

Beaton was a member of the Royalty Protection Command, also known as SO14.

Beaton's mission that night was simple: to ensure the safety and protection of Princess Anne, who was sitting in the backseat with her then-husband, Captain Mark Phillips. Also in the back seat was Anne's lady-in-waiting, Rowena Jane Brassey.

Times were different in the 1970s. Members of the Royal Family today are among the most heavily protected and safeguarded people in the entire world. In the 1970s, they were also well-protected, but not to the extent that they are today. That's because back then, it was believed that there were few serious threats to the Royal Family. Members of the Royal Family would freely travel, with bodyguards, throughout Britain (and the rest of the world, for that matter), and it was very rare that they would be threatened by anyone.

That's why bodyguards of the Royal Family back then received no specific training, and it was common practice for each member of the Royal Family (including the Queen) only to have one bodyguard at a time.

Sure enough, Inspector Beaton was the only officer assigned to protect Princess Anne that night.

Princess Anne had just married Captain Mark Phillips, and the two were worldwide celebrity newlyweds. Even though the level of protection that members of the Royal Family received back then was far lesser than it is today, the amount of global fame, scrutiny, and attention was as extensive as it is today.

Besides the fact that she was the daughter of the Queen, Princess Anne was also famous for being an equestrian. This was how she met Captain Phillips, who was also an equestrian but a commoner. Their wedding was widely broadcast around the world and attracted over half a billion viewers.

On the night of March 20, Princess Anne and her husband were attending a charity film screening. Due to their celebrity status, it was well-known that they would be attending the screening that night. Ian Ball, the man who attacked them, would have had no difficulty finding out where they were.

Ball had been planning a kidnapping and attack on the Royal Family for quite some time. He eventually settled on making his attempt on Anne because he believed she was less well-protected than the other members of the Royal Family.

"I had thought about it for years and she [Anne] would have been the easiest," Ball later told police during the subsequent investigation. "I had seen her riding her horse together with her husband."

Due to the lack of protection and knowing that Anne was vulnerable in the limo on the road, Ball believed she would be an easy target. He would soon find out that he was very wrong…, very wrong.

****

Ball lay in wait and then suddenly pulled his white Ford out in front of the Princess' Rolls-Royce limo to stop it. Callender, the driver, instinctively brought the vehicle to a halt to avoid hitting the Ford.

Beaton, sitting in the front seat next to Callender, initially thought that Ball was simply an angry driver. Callender and Beaton waited for Ball to move his car out of the way, but when Ball got out of the Ford, Beaton also got out to confront him.

Beaton was armed with his service sidearm, a Walther PPK in 7.65mm. The PPK is most famous as the pistol of choice for the fictional British secret service agent James Bond (created by former British intelligence officer Ian Fleming). It is a compact semi-automatic pistol that hides easily and carries seven rounds in the magazine. But while Bond may be a fictional character usually armed with a PPK, Beaton was very much real.

Ball was also armed and more heavily so than Beaton. He had two handguns on him.

As Beaton and Ball walked up to one another, Beaton thought he was in for purely a verbal confrontation. It was only a matter of seconds before he realized that Ball was there for a lot more than that.

Rapidly, Ball withdrew one of the handguns from under his clothing. He took a quick but careful aim at Beaton and fired. One of the bullets struck Beaton directly in the right shoulder and the others shattered the back window of the limo, covering Anne and Phillips in glass.

Beaton recoiled from the impact of the bullet while drawing his PPK from underneath his jacket. He managed to squeeze off a single shot at Ball before the pistol jammed when attempting to cycle in a new round.

Seeing the wounded Beaton attempting to fix his jammed gun and determining he was no longer a serious threat, Ball advanced on the limo. He easily could have dispatched Beaton right then and there, but Ball was more concerned with apprehending the Princess.

He walked over to the limo, gun in hand, and started pulling on the driver's door, which Callender kept shut.

But Beaton was not out of the fight yet. He gave up trying to clear the jam on the Walther and dropped it on the street.

He raced back over to the limo and climbed back into the car. He put his body in between Ball, who was still attempting to open the driver's door, and the Royal couple in the backseat.

Ball could see he had the upper hand. Beaton was disarmed and wounded, and Callender was unarmed and valiantly trying to keep the driver's door shot.

Desperately wanting the Princess, Ball gave up trying to open the driver's door. He turned his pistol to Beaton and shot him again twice, once in the chest and once in the abdomen.

Callender opened the car door to attack Ball, but Ball shot him too, and Callender sank back into the vehicle.

Both Beaton and Ball were now dispatched, and Ball reached inside the vehicle in an attempt to grab Anne and pull her out, but she resisted.

"Please come out!" Ball shouted at Anne as he tugged her out by the arm. "You've got to come!"

To which the Princess sharply replied, "Not bloody likely!"

Phillips grabbed Anne's other arm and attempted to tug her back into the vehicle. The Princess now found herself locked in between the arms of her husband on one side and the assailant on the other.

Her bodyguard and driver were both shot and mortally wounded, and she was seemingly defenseless against her kidnapper.

****

The sound of the gunfire had attracted the attention of a police constable named Michael Hills, who was just 22 years old at the time. Hills would later report that the gunshots sounded like "popping" noises. and he wondered if it was the noise of a malfunctioning vehicle engine.

Following the sound, Hills saw Ball outside the limo. At first, he believed it was a traffic altercation.

Hills approached Ball and tapped him on the arm. Ball released his grip on the Princess inside the limo, turned, and shot Hills directly into the stomach at a near point-blank rage. Hills collapsed onto the ground, but he still managed to get a hold of his radio and alert his fellow officers that he had been shot.

Ball turned back to the Royal couple and demanded that she join him and get into the white Ford, but the Princess sternly refused to comply.

"We had an irritating discussion about where, or where not, we were going to go," she recalled in an interview some years after the attack. "I said I didn't think I wanted to go." Anne tried to keep her attacker talking, later saying, "I was scrupulously polite because I thought it would be silly to be rude at that stage."

The noise of the gunfire and the yelling began to attract the attention of other people. After Hills had gone down, three other bystanders walking along the streets ran up to help.

One of them was Glenmore Martin, a chauffeur, and another was a journalist from the *Daily Mail* named John McConnell.

The third was Ronald Russell, a former boxer.

Martin was the first of these three bystanders to take action. Rather than attack Ball directly, as he saw the gun in his hand, he instead attempted to distract Ball and talk him down.

Ball aimed the gun at Martin, but before he could fire, McConnell appeared and likewise tried to talk Ball down.

"Do not be silly, old boy," said McConnell, "just put the gun down."

Ball said nothing and fired another shot, hitting McConnell in the stomach like Hills and dropping him to the pavement.

As this was happening, Russell snuck up behind Ball and punched him directly in the back of the head just after he had shot McConnell.

Ball attempted to turn his gun on Russell, but thankfully, his shot missed.

Seeing her armed assailant go down, Princess Anne took immediate advantage.

"I could reach the door handle from behind my head, and I opened the door and literally pulled my feet over my head and did a sort of backward somersault onto the road," she later said in an interview.

When Ball saw his prize attempting to run away, he recovered himself to his feet and ran around the car after her. Russell gave chase to Ball and punched him again in the face, dropping him to the pavement yet again.

By now, more police were starting to arrive in squad vehicles. Ball realized that the game was up and that if he wanted to escape, now was his chance.

Wrestling himself free of Russell, he attempted to run away, only to be chased and tackled by a detective named Peter Edmonds. Edmonds disarmed Ball, and more police officers ran up to put Ball in handcuffs.

Princess Anne, who had remained remarkably calm throughout the whole ordeal, later reported that her experience with horses was what enabled her to be so.

"One thing about horses and sport is you have to prepare for the unexpected," she recalled.

The attempted kidnapping by Ian Ball was easily the most unexpected event that Princess Anne had ever experienced in her life and perhaps ever will.

****

Inspector Beaton and Callender survived the ordeal, although both were grievously wounded.

It was Beaton's duty that night to protect Princess Anne, and even though he found himself gunned down and put out of the fight by the assailant, he still did several things right. First and foremost, as soon as he detected the threat in the form of Ball, Beaton wasted no time in getting out of the car to confront him.

And as soon as Beaton could see that Ball was armed and there with malicious intent, he drew his own gun to respond to the fight.

Indeed, perhaps the only reason Beaton was put out of the fight early was because his pistol jammed. Otherwise, he likely would have shot down Ball right then and there.

But even after his gun had jammed and Ball had shot him in the shoulder, Beaton refused to give up on his mission to protect the Princess.

He ran back to put himself in between Ball and the Princess and took another bullet directly to the chest. This alone is an extraordinary and heroic act of personal sacrifice, and it shows how committed and serious Beaton was to his duty.

The fact that Beaton was able to survive his three gunshot wounds is also remarkable.

In fact, everyone who was shot that night would later make a full recovery.

As for Ball, little is known about his motivation for wanting to have kidnapped Princess Anne. In his vehicle, a police search uncovered handcuffs, tranquilizers, and a ransom note demanding two million pounds to be placed in 20 suitcases, as well as a plane to Switzerland after receiving the money.

At his trial, Ball said, "I would like to say that I did it to draw attention to the lack of facilities for treating mental health under the National Health Service."

****

Later, the highest civilian award for courage, the George Cross, was awarded to Inspector Beaton by Queen Elizabeth II.

Meanwhile, the George Medal was presented to Hills and Russell, and Queen's Gallantry Medals were presented to Callender, McConnell, and Edmonds. Martin received the Queen's Commendation for Brave Conduct. Russell later acknowledged that he received gratitude for his actions not as if he had saved the Queen's daughter but just as if he had saved any other mother's daughter.

"The award comes from the queen," he said, "but the thank you comes from Anne's mother."

In 1982, Beaton was promoted to the Queen's Police Officer. He retired in 1992 and enjoys a quiet private life today.

Ball's attack remains the closest that anyone has ever come to kidnapping a member of the British Royal family to this day.

CHAPTER NINE

KEVIN PHILIPPY

"Kung Fu Cop" sounds like the name of a movie.

In reality, it's the name given to a real-life French cop named Kevin Philippy, but maybe one day a movie will indeed be made about Philippy's exploits.

Kevin Philippy was 28 years old and had recently suffered a debilitating injury that forced him to wear a neck brace even while in the line of duty. He was serving as a probationary police officer in Paris when a violent demonstration broke out, and he found himself right in the middle of it.

Little did Philippy know, but soon he and his fellow officers would be under attack from several dangerous and heavily armed protesters equipped with iron bars and Molotov cocktails.

Bravely, Philippy confronted these protestors head-on, using nothing more than his bare hands. Despite his neck injury that severely restricted his movements, he was able to deftly defend himself in hand-to-hand combat against his attacker.

****

Paris may be a city known for romantic restaurants, fine wine, the Eiffel Tower, and scenic views of the River Seine…, and indeed, it has all of these things.

But Paris is not always the calm, charming, and relaxing city that is commonly depicted in movies and media. That's because Paris has also long had a history of violent protests. It was the predominant site of the French Revolution and has witnessed several major social upheavals since then.

In May 2016, police unions were demonstrating across France against the violence that police officers had sustained at the hands of anti-government protesters over the preceding months. The police units claimed that police officers had been suffering "law haine anti-flick" - or anti-cop hatred - for quite some time and that changes to the labor laws were needed.

In response, over 300 people who held far-left or anarchist views held a counter-demonstration against the police officers (despite a ban on counter-demonstrations being put into place) to oppose the police union's proposed law changes.

"COPS, PIGS, KILLERS!" The counter-demonstrators shouted as they marched through the streets.

The situation quickly spiraled out of control and became violent. Iron bars, clubs, and even Molotov cocktails were being deployed as the supporters of the police unions and the counter-demonstrators clashed physically with one another.

A small group of 15 counter-demonstrators surrounded a police traffic patrol car as it was attempting to evade the demonstrations. Each of these demonstrators was masked and hooded to help conceal their identities.

The driver attempted to drive the police car away but was slowed by the people and vehicles surrounding it, it was attacked by those demonstrators who struck the car repeatedly from all angles with bars and clubs.

These attacks smashed the glass on the rear window. One demonstrator even took advantage of this to throw a Molotov cocktail through the back of the car, setting it ablaze from the inside!

Blocked from escape by the cars and protests in front and on fire from the inside, the car came to a slow halt. The driver of the car, a trainee police officer, opened the door and stepped out.

The trainee officer was named Kevin Philippy. He advanced slowly and confidently on the demonstrators attacking the car.

What happened next occurred in only a matter of seconds, but it would show how much the demonstrators had underestimated their opponent.

One hooded demonstrator quickly attacked Philippy, swinging around a metal bar. Philippy, despite having a neck brace that restricted his movement, deftly dodged or deflected each of the attacks by the demonstrator.

The other demonstrators, seeing Philippy's prowess in hand-to-hand fighting, stopped their attack and held themselves at bay.

At one moment, Philippy's right hand dropped down to his side to reach for his SIG Sauer SP2022 9mm duty sidearm, but he thought twice and ultimately opted not to pull it out.

No longer being attacked, Philippy turned and calmly walked away from the burning vehicle to go check on his fellow officer.

****

The entire confrontation between Philippy and the demonstrators was captured on video and amassed tens of millions of views online.

Philippy's superiors in the French police also noticed and praised his defensive efforts.

President Francois Hollande, in a ceremony at the French interior ministry, presented the highest French police award (the Gold Internal Security Medal) to Philippy. Alison Barthelemy, Philippy's fellow officer in the burning vehicle, also received the same award.

Bernard Cazeneuve, the Interior Minister of France, also announced that Philippy would be promoted to 'Guardian of the Peace,' meaning that Philippy would go from being a trainee to a full police officer. This was despite Philippy having recently failed his entrance exam.

"What made me extremely proud was your extreme self-control," Cazeneuve said to Philippy at the event. "Here was a police officer who was strong in his own personality and values, and not just strong because he had a gun."

Philippy, for his part, remained extremely humble during the ceremony.

"Many of my colleagues suffer far worse," he said, "they are the heroes, not me."

Four demonstrators of the group who attacked Philippy were arrested and accused of attempted murder. The four demonstrators were between the ages of 18 and 31 and were identified as being members of a militant anti-fascist group. They were placed under house arrest.

The French media dubbed Philippy the "Kung Fu Police Man" as the footage of what had happened gained national and then worldwide attention.

"The images of the violence they (Kevin Philippy and his colleagues) were subject to will stay etched in the memory of the French people for a long time," Cazeneuve said during the ceremony."

Philippy's excellent self-defense skills are certainly praiseworthy. But even more praiseworthy is the fact that he remained completely calm throughout the whole ordeal, never lost control or went for his handgun when he easily could have, was very brave in confronting the armed demonstrators, showed incredible restraint, and paid very close attention to his fellow police officer to make sure that she was okay.

"After the protests and tensions have passed, we will keep one image in our minds," Cazeneuve continued. "That of a police officer stepping out of a vehicle with one single objective in mind, to protect his colleague."

CHAPTER TEN

LIANG XIAO

Part of the duty of serving as a police officer, regardless of where you are in the world, is to always be ready to save someone's life at a moment's notice.

Sometimes, that duty may mean a police officer needs to put their own life on the line.

Throughout this book thus far, we've observed many stories where police officers have done exactly that. Terrance Yeakey ran into a burning and collapsing building to carry people trapped inside to safety. Rajkamal Meena jumped into a cold river, despite not being very confident in his swimming abilities, to save a boy from drowning.

Mario Gutierrez took multiple stabbings and slashings across his body to stop an arsonist from blowing up a gas station and killing hundreds of people in the area. Donald Thompson put himself into a burning vehicle and sustained numerous first- and second-degree burns to save the person inside.

Not very many people would have the courage to act in these situations. That's why the men and women serving in law enforcement uniforms all over the world are truly among the bravest and most courageous people on the planet.

Next, we're going to read about another police officer who also risked his life to save the life of another. But the way this officer saved the life of a citizen was not through confronting an armed assailant or throwing himself into a burning building or vehicle.

Get ready to read about the story of Liang Xiao.

****

It was 2015 in Nakang Town, Beihai City in southern China. Liang Xiao was a police officer serving there.

It was another ordinary day for Xiao when he and other officers received a call. A suicidal man was standing at the very edge of a four-story high building!

Racing to the site, they looked up to see that a man was indeed standing at the very edge of the building, four stories up.

The officers began pleading with the man to come down from the top of the building, but he refused to heed their commands.

Firefighters arrived at the scene and began preparing equipment to climb up and rescue the man.

Seeing this, the man teetered even closer to the edge of the building. He was still seemingly unsure about throwing himself off of the building, but he also knew that he only had a matter of minutes before firefighters climbed up to rescue him.

Just as the firefighters were preparing the ladders to climb up, the man suddenly jumped.

And when the man jumped, Xiao was the only person who ran forward.

As the man fell, Xiao positioned himself where he expected the man to fall.

He braced himself for the impact, and the man landed right on Xiao and the two collided!

****

Xiao and the other man were alive, but both were badly injured. Xiao had effectively used his body as a shield to cushion the man's fall and save his life, at the risk of his own.

It was amazing that Xiao was still alive, as the force of the falling man caused his own body to fall hard directly over the pavement with the weight of the man pressing down on him.

Xiao suffered a broken left foot, a swollen face, and multiple bruises all over his body, but he was alive. The injuries of the suicidal man who jumped were much less severe, largely because Xiao's body cushioned him from the impact of the fall.

Both Xiao and the then 32-year-old man, who remains unnamed to this day, were rushed to the hospital. The cause for his suicidal attempt was also not revealed.

A passerby filmed the whole incident and uploaded the footage to LiveLeak. The video then spread throughout the internet and gained millions of views from people all over the world.

Xiao was extremely lucky for two primary reasons. The first, and perhaps most obvious reason, is that he did not sustain nearly as much damage to his body as he could have despite the force of the man's body crashing over him.

But the second reason he was lucky is that, in a matter of mere milliseconds, he was able to accurately see where the man would fall and position himself directly under him. Had Xiao's calculations been off by even a few inches, he would not have been able to catch the man.

From the moment the man fell, to the time he crashed over the pavement, was a split second - Xiao must have known he wouldn't even have seconds to act.

In other words, he didn't even have time to think about what he would do. Instead, he just did it. He ran forward, positioned himself where he instinctively believed the man would fall and successfully stopped the fall. He also didn't have time to decide whether he should run forward to stop the man from falling or not.

In many other situations, law enforcement officers may find themselves in situations like Xiao's where they likewise do not have any time to think about and calculate their next move.

If a criminal draws a gun on a police officer, for instance, that officer either has to draw their own gun to return fire or do something to try and get the gun out of the criminal's hand. The officer will have no choice, in a situation like this, to think about what they need to do. Instead, they just have to react quickly and decisively.

For Xiao, this same circumstance applied, but to the case of a suicidal man who jumped from a tall building. Had Xiao been paralyzed even for a second thinking about what he should do, instead of actually doing it, the man certainly would have struck the pavement and died that day.

But because of Xiao's actions, that man who attempted to jump to his death was graced with another chance at life.

CHAPTER ELEVEN

CLARE CHALMERS

Our next true story of police heroism takes us to the Isle of Mull in Scotland. As we'll soon see, this little-known Isle is perhaps the most unlikely of places for a life-or-death incident involving the police to occur.

The Isle of Mull is a small island off the west coast of Scotland. With a population of around 3,000 people, not including the many tourists who visit the Isle each year, Mull is a peaceful environment with four castles and ample opportunities for birdwatching.

The police presence on the Isle of Mull is minimal. The island is served by four police stations, at Bunessan, Craignure, Salen, and Tobermory. However, not all of the police stations are always manned due to the reduced police force on the island. In fact, at certain times, there may be only one or two law enforcement officers on duty for the entire island, depending on the time of the day.

The local police recommend that residents always phone for emergencies. These calls are routed via Oban, a small resort town on the mainland of Scotland before the call is then transferred to the few officers who are on duty.

That being said, life on this little island is usually quiet and it's very rare that any police officers are called up for any serious emergencies or life-threatening incidents. That's why the police presence on Mull has traditionally been kept to the minimum.

If one were told beforehand that this upcoming story of police heroism takes place in Scotland, the Isle of Mull is perhaps the last place they would imagine as the location. But sometimes, the most extraordinary of events can happen in the most unlikely of places.

And that's exactly what happened in September 2020. Life on the Isle of Mull was usually very relaxed and quiet, but it was even more so then because of the Covid-19 pandemic restrictions that were in effect. Most people were heavily limited in where they could move, and the usual influx of tourists hadn't come because of the government shutdowns.

Life on Mull had largely been boring and uneventful for the whole year. That was, until PC Clare Chalmers, one of the few police officers serving on the Isle of Mull, received the last call she ever wanted to get, at the end of a very long and tiring shift.

****

Chalmers had just worked a long 10-hour shift and was on her way home when she received the call from the police department at Oban. They were reporting a violent incident that was occurring at a nearby residence on the island.

This by itself was highly unusual because incidents involving the police in peaceful Mull were usually relegated to parking tickets or drunk patrons at the pubs. This case was different because it was a case of domestic violence occurring at a private residence.

The first thing Chalmers did was to call in for backup from other members of the team. Unfortunately, there was only one other police officer on duty, and since they were on the other side of the Isle, they could not get to the residence quickly.

This meant that Chalmers was forced to respond to the incident on her own. The 55-year-old woman would have to go up against a man much bigger and more formidable than her - without any assistance or help from another officer.

On top of that, Chalmers was already exhausted from her shift. Before receiving the call, she'd just wanted to go home to eat dinner and sleep to get enough rest before continuing again the next day.

Tired and alone, she'd be going up against a violent person much bigger than she was and with no hope for imminent backup.

The thought of such a precarious situation would have dissuaded many police officers, but undeterred, Chalmers barreled down the road to the residence in her police vehicle.

When she arrived at the residence and got out of her police vehicle, she found a sobbing woman by the house with a very bloodied face.

Through tears and blood, as Chalmers comforted her, the woman managed to get out that she had just been violently attacked by a man who was still on the property. The man was armed with a knife and had slashed the woman's face multiple times - she'd be left with scars for the rest of her life.

The man was still inside her house, as far as the woman knew.

Chalmers had two choices now. She could either wait for the other officer to arrive or she could enter the house to search for the man and try to arrest him.

She knew that there was substantial risk to her own life if she entered the home. She also knew that there was a greater risk to other people if she failed to apprehend the violent man now. If she let him escape, he could go and attack someone else.

At that moment, Chalmers decided to enter. Even though she wasn't much bigger than the wounded woman who had just had her face slashed by this man - and knowing she carried the same risk of the same thing (or worse) happening to her - Chalmers knew that she couldn't risk the man getting away.

It's this kind of quick and decisive thinking, and specifically, the act of putting the lives of other people they are sworn to protect ahead of their own, that police officers need to practice in extreme circumstances, and Chalmers demonstrated it that day.

With a balance of caution and determination, Chalmers entered the home. She carefully searched the entrance, kitchen, living room, and bathrooms, but the home appeared mysteriously empty. She couldn't hear anyone in the home either, and no one responded when she called out, even though the wounded woman had insisted the man was there somewhere.

Where was he?

****

Chalmers then entered a bedroom and discovered someone hiding, rather poorly, under the blanket on the bed.

Immediately, Chalmers called for whoever was hiding under the blanket to reveal themselves. Her hand dropped to the case of PAVA spray that she kept on her side.

PAVA, or Pelargonic Acid Vanillylamide, Spray is a self-defense spray very similar to pepper spray in that it's designed to incapacitate an attacker. Propelled by nitrogen, the solution in PAVA has an effective range of 13 feet (although the best accuracy is achieved within six feet) and is designed to inflict severe pain on the victim's eyes and cause them to close instantly.

The person under the blankets revealed himself as a very large and intimidating man…, and he was armed with two knives!

Chalmers realized that this was indeed the man who had attacked the woman outside. Without even thinking about it, she instinctively drew the PAVA Spray from her belt and held it in front of her while ordering the man with a loud and firm voice to drop both blades.

The man looked at Chalmers with both of the knives in his hands. He was standing mere feet away from her, and he could charge her at any minute. This was well within the effective range of the PAVA, but Chalmers would only have one opportunity to spray him in the face before he reached her with his weapons.

If he attacked, Chalmers' life was entirely dependent on whether she could incapacitate him before he reached her. It was very possible that she could miss, or that the PAVA would fail to stop him before he got to her - ready to give her the same or worse fate as the wounded woman outside.

"Drop the knives!" Chalmers continued to yell at the man. "Drop them!"

Only seconds had passed since Chalmers had discovered the man, and yet to her, it felt like an eternity.

"Drop them!" Chalmers shouted again, her heart pounding in anticipation of what the man would do.

Suddenly, without a word, the man charged forward. Chalmers fired the PAVA canister, hurling a spray of acid directly into the man's face and eyes!

She backed up rapidly as she sprayed to avoid the knife blades. The man screamed in pain, missed her with the knives, and collapsed to the floor in agony, clutching his face.

Chalmers instantly disarmed the man of his knives. She then drew her handcuffs to detain him.

Returning outside, Chalmers called in a helicopter for backup and returned to the wounded woman to comfort her further. The detained suspect remained inside the home - still yelling threats and obscenities at the two women.

Chalmers then set up a police cordon around the house and property to block it off from other people.

The helicopter called in from the Scottish coastline flew in to apprehend the man. Later in court, he would plead guilty and receive a sentence of eight months in prison.

****

The incident attracted attention in the media and newspapers throughout the United Kingdom. At a time when people were spending most of their time at home doing nothing due to the restrictions, the confrontation between Chalmers and the violent man on the usually peaceful Isle of Mull was a bit of a shock.

What rightfully received the most attention in the incident was the sheer bravery that Chalmers demonstrated throughout the whole event. She knew full well that she would be at a significant disadvantage in confronting any armed and violent man without backup, and yet she confronted him anyway, without a second thought. She knew it was her duty to put herself in between him and anyone else who he could hurt.

Chalmers also demonstrated extreme restraint and used violent force at the end only when there was no other recourse. She called out numerous times for the man to stop and drop his knives, and she unloaded the PAVA spray into his face only once he attacked and closed in on her.

A spokesman for Police Scotland would later say of Chalmers: "Clare's instinctive and courageous actions resulted in the arrest of a violent offender who subsequently received a custodial sentence."

Chalmers continued to do the right thing even after the man was apprehended. After handcuffing him, she set up a perimeter around the house to block it off from anyone else. Many people in the neighborhood were alerted to the incident from the noise, but Chalmers made sure that no one else entered the house.

It's worth noting as well that Chalmers was also extremely lucky. If she missed, or the PAVA failed to stop her attacker, the final outcome could have been a lot more gruesome than it ended up being.

In short, Chalmers acted with the right balance of decisiveness, courage, and restraint that a police officer needs to show while in the line of duty. She was the hero of Scotland that day.

****

Chalmers was one of eight officers recognized by the Scottish Police Federation's awards ceremony that year. Hosted annually in Edinburgh, the ceremony honors Scottish police officers who go above and beyond what is expected of them.

The eight officers who won the awards were selected from more than 100 nominations for the year.

"Every minute of every day, Police Scotland officers step forward with bravery, compassion and professionalism to protect their fellow citizens," said Chief Constable Iain Livingstone at the event. "I thank and pay tribute to our officers and their families for their commitment and public service. I am grateful to the Scottish Police Federation for underlining and recognizing the courage and excellence demonstrated by police officers in Scotland to keep people safe."

In response to receiving the award, the humility Chalmers reacted with was at the same level as the bravery she had demonstrated in apprehending the violent offender.

"I was only doing what any other police officer would do in my position and I would do it again in a heartbeat," she said. "My job is to protect. I feel truly humbled by this award."

CHAPTER TWELVE

WAYNE MARQUES

This story of police heroism takes us right into the heart of London. On June 3, 2017, a terrorist attack was carried out in this megacity that sent shockwaves all across the United Kingdom.

A van was driven deliberately into people walking across London Bridge before crashing into Borough High Street by the River Thames. The occupants of the vans then ran out of the vehicle and began attacking people with knives in the surrounding restaurants and pubs before they were stopped by police.

Eight people were tragically killed and nearly 50 were injured, including four police officers who acted to stop the terrorists. The terrorist group ISIS later claimed responsibility for the attack.

The attack was actually one of five major terrorist attacks carried out in the UK in 2017. Another vehicle and knife attack had occurred just three months earlier at Westminster, and only a couple of weeks prior, a suicide bomber killed more than 20 people at a concert in Manchester.

As a result of the Manchester attack, the terror threat level had been raised to 'Critical'. It was amazing and distressing to many that London, one of the largest and most safeguarded cities in the entire Western world, had become a targeted hotspot for terrorists.

But even though the Manchester suicide bombing had been terrible, the worst was not over yet. When the June 3 incident occurred almost directly after what happened in Manchester, it made many people wonder if the attacks in the UK would ever end.

The attackers in London on June 3 acquired a white Renault van to carry out their assault and armed themselves with 12-inch long, ceramic-bladed knives. They tied these knives to their wrists with leather straps to ensure they would be easily accessible. They also wrapped fake explosive belts around themselves by covering water bottles in gray-colored tape to make it appear as if they were explosives.

Late at night, the soon-to-be attackers drove the white van over London Bridge. They made a U-turn and came back onto the bridge. Suddenly accelerating, the van veered from the main road onto the pavement and struck multiple people who were walking over the bridge!

Two were killed instantly and several more were badly hurt. The dozens of other people walking along the bridge ran in all directions in an attempt to evade the barreling van.

People quickly began dialing 999 emergency calls to alert law enforcement.

The van returned to the opposite end of the bridge, toward Borough High Street, presumably to run over more people. Thankfully, it crashed en route when its tires were destroyed.

The three attackers, drawing their knives from their wrists, abandoned the vehicle and ran to Greek Dragon Court, where they started attacking people who were in the restaurants and pubs dining. Five people were killed from stab wounds, and dozens more were brutally slashed and stabbed and would end up in critical condition in the hospital.

The attack was a fierce frenzy; the terrorists almost had free reign to stab as many people and inflict as much damage as they could. Many people attempted to fight back in an attempt to give others a chance to escape but being unarmed, there was little they could do but minimize the carnage.

Police officers started to arrive on the scene, but they were unarmed and had to confront the attackers with nothing more than their bare hands. The terrorists had the advantage, but it was because of the efforts of those police officers that further loss of life was prevented.

One particular London police officer who came to the rescue of people that fateful day was named Wayne Marques.

****

The terrorists were moving "like a wolf pack", Marques would later recall when he talked about what he witnessed and experienced during the attack in Borough Market.

And he was certainly right: the only thing the people in Borough Market could do was run like deer in the face of an attack by a wolf pack.

Marques was on patrol near London Bridge that night. He first caught wind of the attack when he heard a woman's scream. Turning his attention to where the noise was coming from, he saw dozens of people running out of Borough High Street in an absolute state of panic.

Knowing that something was very wrong, Marques ran over to investigate. Entering the High Street, he saw some people running for their lives and others standing still "looking like statues" as if "they were rabbits caught in a headlight."

Everyone was terrified of what was happening, and some were expressing their terror by running away, while others were so petrified with fear that they couldn't move.

"What is going on?" Marques thought over and over again.

He found himself running against the flow of the crowd to seek the source of everyone's torment.

Marques' arm was grabbed by another man who was running with the crowd.

"Mate, mate this guy's been stabbed!" The man yelled, pointing Marques' attention to the bloodied body of a man lying still on the ground.

Marques later found out that the bloodied man on the ground had been stabbed multiple times in the head and neck. His name was Oliver Dowling (thankfully, he would survive the attack and corroborate the story of Marques' heroism afterwards).

Oliver's girlfriend, Marie Bondeville, was also severely wounded from multiple stab wounds. She was standing over him, sobbing and screaming, when another man suddenly came up behind her and punched her to the ground. Marie went down, and then he grabbed her head and yanked her back up with one hand and a knife in the other. The man was one of the terrorists from the white van!

"Hey!" Marques shouted as his hand dropped to the baton that he kept on his duty belt at his hip.

Besides his stab vest that he always wore while on patrol, the only defensive weapon that Marques had on him was that baton. He had no knife and no firearm.

Despite being under-armed, Marques knew that he had to act instantly if he was going to save Marie's life and get Oliver to medical help in time. With the baton in hand, he charged the terrorist.

Turning his attention to Marques and letting go of Marie, the terrorist with the knife charged in turn to meet him.

"My intention was to hit him as hard as I could with all my weight behind me with everything I had," Marques recalled, "I knew he was trying to kill the man on the floor."

The two men closed in on one another. Marques got in the first blow and struck the terrorist right across the forehead. The terrorist staggered back, his knife still in hand, and Marques followed up his attack with a punch to the terrorist's face that sent him staggering back further.

Suddenly, out of the corner of his right eye, Marques saw the blade of a knife flash into view, followed by massive pain that shot out of his forehead.

Darkness overtook his right eye, and he reeled back in pain and shock.

While he had been striking blows to the first terrorist attacking Oliver and Marie, a second terrorist had joined in on the fight and slashed Marques across his forehead right above his right eye.

"I was aware that I was being stabbed and cut, but did not really feel the pain as such," said Marques, "when fighting for your life, the adrenaline has taken over."

Marques instinctively backed up to avoid more slashings from the second terrorist, and it was then he noticed a third terrorist, also armed with a knife, arriving on the scene.

"Allahu akbar!" The new terrorist was shouting numerous times. "Allahu akbar! Allahu akbar!"

Marques suddenly realized that he was not facing down one attacker but two, and then not two but three. And all three were armed. Furthermore, he could tell that the terrorists were well-trained and knew what they were doing. All three men were fighting in a coordinated fashion and attacking him from different angles "like a wolf pack."

Despite being heavily outnumbered and under-armed, Marques resolved right then and there to stop all three attackers before more police officers could arrive to assist him. He could already tell they had killed or wounded many people on High Street, and he was the only police officer on the scene.

It was his duty to confront all three men and stop them dead in their tracks…, or else go down trying himself.

"I decided to hold on and keep them fighting until the cavalry arrived," Marques would later say, "I ended up having this voice in my head just telling me 'don't go down, don't go down.'"

It was this voice in his head that kept Marques going. He was bleeding profusely from the wound above his right eye, and his vision in that eye was almost completely gone. But he could still see out of his left eye, and he still had the baton in his hand.

The three terrorists surrounded Marques but kept their distance.

Then, suddenly, all three of the terrorists closed in. They struck forward with their knives and slashed or stabbed Marques multiple times all over his body, his front and his back.

"They were going to kill me," Marques would say later.

Despite his body getting stabbed and slashed more than a dozen times, Marques fought back valiantly. He swung against the terrorists with his baton, striking them multiple times, but each time he would strike one terrorist, another would come up behind him and stab him in the back. Then Marques would turn to defend himself against that terrorist, only to get struck again by another.

It was three against one, and Marques was losing. It was either him or them, and the thought crossed his mind that it may end up being him who would go down that night.

Suddenly, shots rang out. The terrorists stopped their attack on Marques and scattered.

Despite his vision being in a very poor state, Marques was able to look up and see some other London police officers, armed with automatic rifles and handguns.

The cavalry had arrived like Marques had been hoping. The tide had now turned against the terrorists with the arrival of the reinforcements.

The gunfire continued to ring out around Marques as the new police officers shot at the fleeing terrorists.

Then the shooting abruptly stopped. All three of the terrorists had been shot and were now on the ground themselves.

Even though he was lying on the ground in a growing pool of his own blood, Marques was relieved.

The attack was over.

****

That attack on London Bridge that night in June 2017 was horrific for the people of London, a tragic event that the population of that city will never forget.

The rampage of the terrorists from their first attack in the van on London Bridge to when they were finally gunned down by law enforcement lasted a total of 10 minutes. Forty-six bullets were fired by five London police officers to bring an end to the lives of those terrorists.

Eight people were killed and nearly 50 were wounded, but it could have been a lot more had it not been for the efforts of Wayne Marques.

Even though Marques was unable to stop the terrorists by himself, which is understandable since he was outnumbered and under-armed, he successfully held them off. This bought enough time for people to escape before armed police officers arrived to shoot down the terrorists and end it.

Marques was not the only police officer brutally wounded that night either. Before they had come to Marques, the trio of terrorists had attacked police officer Charlie Guenigault, who happened to stumble into the attack while he was walking home. He took two stab wounds to his back and his head before the terrorists pressed on to continue their rampage.

Immediately following the attack, all of the buildings within the general area of London Bridge were evacuated on the orders of the police. Even though the three terrorists were shot down, there was no way of knowing if they were the only terrorists in the area or if further attacks were planned. The UK had been the target of numerous attacks that year, and the police could take no chances.

A military counter-terrorist unit from the SAS (Special Air Service) was deployed as well. Joining forces with the Metropolitan Police, they conducted a wide search on and around London Bridge to look for any further casualties and to assist with the evacuation efforts.

Marques went to the hospital after the attack and made a full recovery, with his vision completely restored.

****

A ceremony to honor the bravery of those who acted with courage at both the London Bridge and the earlier Manchester attacks was held at the National Rail Awards in September of that year.

Transport Secretary Chris Grayling recognized Marques for his heroic efforts to help stop the terrorists.

"We are hugely fortunate to have a dedicated team of officers, fantastically-led, who do a brilliant job for this industry and I think we all owe them a huge debt of gratitude," said Grayling in commendation of Marques and the other British law enforcement officers who played a hand in stopping the terrorists that night. "Transport police officers and station staff went above and beyond the call of duty when handling the aftermath of the terror attacks in both Manchester and London Bridge this year."

Marques was willing to give his life to stop those terrorists from murdering more people…, and he almost did give his life. Even though he sustained grievous wounds and nearly lost an eye, he delayed the terrorists until other police officers arrived to put an end to the terrorist attack.

In other words, the 2017 attack on London Bridge would have been a far worse and more tragic catastrophe without the courage Marques displayed.

Thankfully, Marques survived the horrible wounds, and he's still serving London to this day. He's yet another excellent example of a law enforcement officer willing to go above and beyond the call of duty at a moment's notice to save members of the public.

It's police officers with the same character and bravery as Marques that allow us to stay safe while going about our daily lives in public, by stopping dangerous criminals when they try to inflict harm or death upon us or those we love.

Without the efforts of brave officers in uniform like him, it's simply unfathomable how much more dangerous life could be.

CHAPTER THIRTEEN

CHAD MCCOY

A cop always has to be ready to act while on duty. But sometimes a cop has to be ready to act *off-duty* too.

That was the case for Utah Highway Patrol Officer Chad McCoy in April 2023.

It was mid-afternoon and McCoy, a 12-year veteran on the force, had just finished his shift in Salt Lake County. He was heading back to his home in an adjoining county. He was still in uniform and driving his patrol cruiser, however.

While driving along the interstate, McCoy noticed something very strange. Each of the vehicles along the opposite side of the road were moving right as if they were trying to avoid something that was oncoming.

Looking ahead, he quickly became alarmed as he saw a pickup truck heading down the wrong lane!

"I didn't hear anything on the police radio at that time," McCoy would later recall, "I just noticed ahead of me cars moving to the right, and then I saw this truck that was facing the wrong direction and then I realized that it was actually traveling at a pretty high rate of speed."

McCoy made the split-second decision to intervene. And his way of intervening? To hit the truck nearly head-on!

****

McCoy would later find out that emergency dispatchers had alerted troopers in the vicinity to look out for a pickup truck that was headed east on a westbound lane. Even though he was already in the area, McCoy didn't hear the broadcast.

The moment McCoy saw the truck coming barreling down the wrong lane, he switched on his blue and red emergency lights. McCoy hoped that even if it didn't stop the truck driver, it would at least alert the other drivers on the road to pull over and get out of the way.

As the pickup truck approached, McCoy slowed his patrol vehicle down to around 15 miles per hour. As the accelerating pickup truck was racing up next to him, McCoy turned his steering wheel sharply.

The front driver's side of McCoy's vehicle struck the driver's side of the pickup truck. The purpose of this, McCoy would later say, was to avoid a head-on collision that would have almost certainly resulted in death for both him and the truck driver.

"We often talk about playing the 'What if?' game," McCoy would later say. "What if this or that were to happen to you? Because we know in those situations where we only have seconds to act, we don't have time to think things through. So, I think a lot of the preparation happens before the moment that it happens. So, in those few seconds, it's just more of a reflex than a long thought process."

The two vehicles collided with one another and came to a stop. McCoy took a few seconds to process that he was alright, and then he got out of his vehicle to check on the driver of the pickup truck.

The driver turned out to be a 62-year-old man. More police officers and an ambulance arrived at the scene in a matter of minutes, and both McCoy and the driver were taken to the nearest hospital as a precautionary measure. McCoy was sore for several days after the attack, but he was back on the job after a week. The pickup driver's reason for driving so fast in the wrong lane was not disclosed.

****

Law enforcement in the state heavily praised McCoy's actions.

Colonel Michael Rapich, the Head of the Utah Highway Patrol unit, was quick to do so publicly.

"We're incredibly proud of him," McCoy said. "We're incredibly grateful that he's OK and wasn't hurt. And we're grateful no one else was hurt as a result of this incident…, when crashes involving wrong-way drivers occur, they're violent, tragic, and horrible. And they represent a significant threat to the motorists in the state of Utah."

Even the Governor of Utah, Spencer Cox, put out a tweet praising McCoy's actions: "This trooper had just finished his shift and was on his way home when he saw a car coming at him going the wrong way. He knew he had one chance to protect the drivers behind him. Without hesitation, he put his own life on the line. I'm grateful for heroes."

It's extremely difficult for police officers to contend with the predicament of wrong-lane drivers. The standard procedure for police troopers is to stop all other traffic and then have another officer stop the wrong-way driver with the precision immobilization technique (PIT).

This is a tactic in which a pursuing police vehicle forces another vehicle in front of it to turn sideways, causing the driver to lose control of the vehicle and stop.

In McCoy's case, however, he was facing the pickup driver directly, so he was unable to use this maneuver. McCoy also didn't have time to call on other police officers to get into position.

McCoy did two things right in this situation. First, he took matters into his own hands to stop the wrong-lane driver. He put his own life on the line to protect the lives of the other drivers on the road.

Second, McCoy thought about *how* he would stop the wrong-lane driver. McCoy was smart enough to know that a head-on collision could prove fatal to both him and the driver. He understood that hitting the driver at an angle would be a safer way to stop him. McCoy's quick-thinking hypothesis was proven correct as both he and the pickup driver emerged from the crash unscathed other than some soreness.

McCoy said that he was most grateful that he could return home to his wife of 12 years, Nicole, and their four children. Nicole likewise was beyond grateful that her husband survived the crash.

"Just seeing him, I just wanted to hug him," Nicole said when McCoy returned home from the hospital.

Today, McCoy is back on duty, working to protect the people of Utah.

"I just see myself as a regular trooper," McCoy said, "I really think we all have that mindset. We come to work every day, just trying to keep people safe."

CHAPTER FOURTEEN

NICKOLAS WILT

The day a new police officer is formally sworn in is the day that officers' commitment to their duty begins.

For 26-year-old Nickolas Wilt, the moment he had to risk his life and confront a violent criminal to save others came only two weeks after he was sworn into the Louisville Metro Police Department.

****

On April 10, 2023, a massive tragedy struck the Old National Bank of Louisville, Kentucky.

Early in the morning, a 25-year-old man walked right into the first floor of the bank holding a semi-automatic rifle.

At that time, the managers and several employees of the bank were gathered together in the conference room on the first floor for the morning meeting. Each of the employees was physically present except for one manager, Rebecca Buchheit-Sims, who had joined the meeting remotely via FaceTime.

The meeting was moving ahead as planned and at first, it was just like any other morning executive meeting at the bank.

Then, suddenly, Rebecca heard loud popping noises coming through the microphone. Startled, she looked at her screen, and to her horror, she could see her fellow employees getting up and starting to run. And then, only seconds later, more were falling over in sprays of blood.

It took a moment for what was happening to dawn on Rebecca: she was watching a mass shooting unfold on camera - and the victims were her fellow employees who she had come to know and love during her career at the bank.

And the worst part about it? There was nothing she could do except sit and watch it unfold!

"I'm still in just as much shock and disbelief and was in disbelief as I watched it unravel," she would later say.

Even worse, the shooter (who won't be named in this book) began to live stream the shooting on Instagram. The livestream continued to run until it was taken down by Instagram after the shooting was over.

Within seconds of the incident beginning, the Louisville police received reports of shots fired and a possible active shooter situation.

Within three minutes, the officers nearest to the bank arrived in their squad vehicles and ran out to engage the shooter.

One of those officers was Nickolas Wilt.

****

The shooter was firing his rifle rapidly when the officers arrived with their pistols drawn, Wilt in the lead.

A rapid volley of gunfire was exchanged between the police officers and the lone gunman.

When it was over, the gunman was on the ground and dead. But Wilt was on the ground too. He had been shot in the head.

Wilt should have been dead, as he had been shot directly in the head by a high-velocity rifle bullet. But he was alive. Despite losing blood fast, he held on as his fellow police officers got to work to try and slow the flow of the bleeding. Soon, an ambulance and emergency first responders arrived.

They transported Wilt to the nearest hospital. There he was connected to an extracorporeal membrane oxygenation machine, which worked to pump blood throughout his body. Wilt would remain hooked to this machine for the next 48 hours.

At the hospital, Wilt became afflicted with pneumonia and a serious lung infection, throwing his chances of recovery into serious doubt as he stayed hooked onto a ventilator to help him stay alive.

Wilt's family visited and prayed for him daily. He was closely monitored by doctors. He was unconscious for much of his recovery, and the news of him coming down with pneumonia didn't exactly lift anybody's spirits.

But Wilt just wouldn't die. He kept holding on. When he was awake, he had a very hard time communicating and responding to commands, and he would slip in and out of consciousness.

Meanwhile, a vigil was held in Louisville, where a crowd collectively prayed for Wilt's recovery. They celebrated each step forward in his recovery.

Wilt had the full support of his family, the doctors, his fellow police officers, and the Louisville community at his back. And it was this support that just may have been what saved his life.

****

One month after the shooting, Wilt was feeling better physically and understanding verbal commands well enough that he could be transferred from the hospital to a neurological rehab facility.

The Louisville Metro Police Department continued to provide their full support to Wilt, releasing a statement stating, "Nick will keep fighting while we continue to keep praying."

The department also held a fundraiser where they collected nearly $165,000 to help cover Wilt's medical expenses.

Wilt's amazing story of recovery reminds us of two fundamental things. The first thing is that the police officer never gets to choose when they may have to go and put their life on the line. In Wilt's case, this moment came no less than two weeks after being sworn in.

But he didn't let his youth or inexperience get in his mind or slow him down. When Wilt responded to the gunfire, he led the other officers into that building to engage the shooter. Wilt rose that day to the level of courage that any police officer needs to display in extraordinary circumstances like that.

Secondly, it shows the support from loved ones and their departments that police officers should receive when they are severely injured in the line of duty. Wilt had full support and prayers from his family, his department, and his community throughout his miraculous recovery process and that undoubtedly played a role in his survival.

CHAPTER FIFTEEN

RAYMON WASHINGTON

Throughout this book, we have covered many real-life stories about police officers who went up against violent assailants and either apprehended them or were violently injured in the process of attempting to do so.

Here, we have a slightly different kind of story, but one that's no less inspirational. That's because this story involves a cop who was violently injured by an assailant…, but instead of shooting the assailant dead or ensuring he was sent to prison for a long time, he became friends with and mentored him instead.

It was the summer of 2020 in Miami, Florida. Protests had erupted all over the nation in response to cultural upheavals, and Miami was not spared from this disorder.

Seventeen-year-old Michael Marshall decided on June 10 to join a Black Lives Matter (BLM) protest for the first time in his life. Michael wasn't even a legal adult yet but at six foot four inches, he was still a formidable figure.

He had grown up in Miami and was the youngest child of a single mother named Josephine Marshall, a retired nursing assistant. He also had an older sister and a young nephew.

Michael recalled that he had lived a rather sheltered childhood. He preferred individual sports such as skateboarding to team-based sports. But because of his sheer size, he joined his high school's football team anyway.

Michael also spent a lot of his time on social media, and when the protests began to break out that year over race relations and he kept a close eye on what was going on.

Soon, rallies were being held daily all over Florida, but Miami's protests remained rather calm and nonviolent compared to what was going on in other cities in the country. Michael wanted to join and take part in a protest, but he also wanted to avoid violence. Since Miami's protests were mostly peaceful and close to where he was, he decided it was the perfect time to go.

Josephine dropped Michael off by Bayside Marketplace. From there, Michael set out on foot to go join the protests.

Michael had his reasons for doing so. He would later say: "It was important to me as a young Black man to go out there and stand with my people. It was important to represent something way bigger than me."

However, the particular BLM protest that he joined ended up becoming way more violent than he had expected as emotions in the crowd flared. Demonstrators, chanting and waving signs, began to openly vandalize the statues of Christopher Columbus and Juan Ponce de Leon.

In response, the Miami Police Department deployed a platoon to counter the demonstrators. One of those police officers was named Raymon Washington.

Soon, the fates of Washington and Michael would intertwine in a way the two did not expect.

****

Twenty-seven-year-old Raymon Washington was a short and slender officer who was deployed along with his twin brother, Jayson. The two brothers both served in law enforcement because of their family's history. Their father and grandfather were both retired cops.

Washington had grown up in Broward County. In his youth, he was a skilled athlete who did well in swimming, running track, and football. While he was playing football in high school and college, Washington sustained multiple concussions from far larger players who would crash into him during play. He was a tough man who could take a lot of physical abuse despite his small size.

Enrolling in the Miami Police Academy in 2015, Washington excelled in his classes, but the effects of the concussions he sustained from his football years gave him trouble. The sunlight would often cause him to have big headaches and hurt his eyes, which is why he preferred to work nighttime shifts as a police officer.

When the June BLM protests broke out in 2020, Washington was sympathetic to the cause.

'The uproar, I understood it..., there is change that needs to happen but tearing up the city is not one way," Washington would later say.

When Washington arrived at the protests on that fateful day, it wasn't exactly just another day in the office.

Police sirens were blaring. Demonstrators were chanting and waving signs. Statues were being vandalized. Skateboards were being smashed over the door of police vehicles. People screamed at officers and Washington himself got into a physical altercation with one of the protestors.

While he was grappling with the protester, another protester brought his skateboard crashing down over Washington's head.

The man who had struck Washington was Michael, who despite not having planned on going to a violent protest, had gotten caught up in the emotions and the actions of the other protestors.

The video footage of the incident is from so far away that it's difficult to see.

Despite this, the footage soon found its way all over social media, being shared and re-shared around the country. Of course, no one else in the country knew that these men were Raymon Washington and Michael Marshall. They just saw a police officer and a protestor at a rally that had turned violent.

****

Michael regretted his actions as he was headed back home.

"When I was going home, I looked around and realized this took a hard curve and it wasn't for me," he would say.

After the protest was over, Washington was still on duty when his head began to throb horribly. Soon, nausea and then vomiting sent in. Another police officer showed Washington the footage of Michael striking him. He decided to return home, knowing that he had sustained a concussion.

"I took a shower, ordered a pizza and slept for three days," Washington said. "I woke up to my brother kicking in my front door. They thought I was dead."

Meanwhile, Michael surrendered himself to the authorities a few days after the incident. Video footage of the incident was circulating widely online, and it didn't take long for the police to identify who he was. Michael faced a charge of aggravated battery of a police officer.

Five months later, however, something changed.

Michael was filled with remorse over his actions of hitting Washington, and he was involved in a brutal legal battle. His attorney, Julian Stroleny, was working hard to get a plea deal that would ensure Michael would continue to have a clean record so he could play football.

"The young man before me was kind, timid, humble, and incredibly remorseful," Stroleny recalled, "he had no priors, excellent grades, and was a star athlete. Not even detention at school."

As part of the plea deal, Stroleny proposed to Michael that he meet with Washington.

When Washington received the invitation, his initial reaction was a firm 'No.'

On top of simply not wanting to meet the teenager who had struck him over the head and accelerated and made the effects of his concussions worse, he didn't want to deal with the juvenile justice system, an arena with which he had very little experience.

He changed his mind, however, when he received another invitation from the Marshall family and also learned about Michael's football aspirations and the fact that those aspirations could be derailed by the likely upcoming record of battery.

Though he wasn't sure about what he was getting into, Washington agreed to meet with Michael, Stroleny, and members of the Marshall family.

After everyone had exchanged greetings and sat down, Michael proceeded to give a three-page apology letter to Washington, which brought the police officer to tears as he read it.

"I was that kid, a high school athlete who wanted to go to college and had offers on the table," Washington later said. "I was like, I don't want to screw this kid up. If I can change one life, and that's it, then that's it."

Washington then explained his history of concussions and how the blow sustained from Michael swinging his skateboard had made his headaches and eye pain much worse. This devastated Michael.

At the end of their emotional meeting, Washington gave Michael his phone number and offered to arrange tutoring and rides to and from football practice.

Washington and Michael continued to communicate and text one another. They talked about their lives, families, and football. Eventually, the Marshall family invited Washington over to meet them, and Washington sat in the stands with them to watch one of Michael's games.

In that game, Michael scored two sacks and five tackles to help his team win the game.

"I played amazing, he was so proud of me," Michael said.

Later, Michael's attorney reached a plea deal with the state of Florida that received the full blessing of Washington. The deal was set so that if Michael completed his volunteer hours and probation with the Miami Police Department, his record would be expunged two years later at the age of 19.

Today, Washington and Michael are still close friends.

CHAPTER SIXTEEN

MAURICE J. 'CULLY' CULLINANE

In March 1977, a hostage-taking terrorist attack rocked the city of Washington D.C. Twelve armed members of the Hanafi Movement, an Islamic extremist group based out of the city, seized control of three buildings (the B'nai B'rith headquarters, District Building, and the Islamic Center of Washington).

The assailants were commanded by Hamaas Abdul Khaalis. He made several demands of the authorities, including access to the killers of his family and those of Malcolm X (presumably so he could execute them), and for the premier of a film entitled *Mohammad, Messenger of God* to be canceled because he considered it to be sacrilegious.

Seven of the 12 terrorists in Khaalis' group entered the headquarters at B'nai B'rith and took 100 hostages. An hour later, three more armed men went into the Islamic Center of

Washington, where they took 11 hostages. And then not long after that, two more terrorists entered the District Building just a few blocks away from the White House.

Police surrounded the buildings from the outside to lay siege.

In the District Building, the hostage takers opened fire with their guns and shot down Maurice Williams, a WHUR-FM radio reporter who tried to verbally engage with the terrorists in the hallway and get access to them via an elevator. Williams died almost instantly, while a D.C. police officer accompanying Williams to meet with the terrorist named Mack Cantrell was fatally wounded (he would tragically die several days later).

Future D.C. Mayor and then-councilman Marion Barry entered the hallway after hearing the gunfire and was struck by ricochet shotgun pellets that lodged just above his heart. Barry was thankfully able to avoid being taken hostage himself and was extracted to a hospital where he recovered.

At this stage in the crisis, the terrorists had the upper hand. But that was about to change. Khaalis and his gang were about to go up against one of the most respected police chiefs in D.C.'s history: Maurice J. 'Cully' Cullinane.

****

Cully had become the chief of the D.C. police in 1974. A native of the city, he served in the United States Navy during the Korean War before following in the footsteps of his father and great uncles by joining the Washington D.C. police force in 1955.

Known for his soft-spoken nature combined with his natural assertiveness, Cully rose through the ranks and gained the respect of his superiors on the force. In late 1974, the Mayor of D.C., Walter E. Washington, asked Cully to serve as the city's new chief of police. Cully accepted.

One of Cully's priorities as chief was to help rebuild the city from the immense devastation it had sustained during the 1968 riots. When those riots had taken place, Cully had been serving as a police lieutenant and ensured the officers serving under his command did not open fire on demonstrators and those involved in the chaos that had enveloped the city.

This was part of how Cully gained a reputation as a leader with a calm and steady hand and why his superiors recommended him to become the next police chief when the time came.

Cully also gained national attention for calling for a community-based policing model, or a policing strategy that revolves around police and community members collaborating to identify and fix problems, essentially turning the police and the community into allies to ensure the safety of neighborhoods. This view was later described as being ahead of its time.

The biggest trial of Cully's career, however, came during that fateful day in 1977. When the Washington D.C. police surrounded and laid siege to the three buildings with the terrorists and the hostages, Cully was right there in the center of it all.

****

Throughout the negotiations, the steady yet assertive approach to dealing with problems that Cully had become known for was evident. He was not the highest-ranking official there, but he was the one leading the negotiations.

The White House and government agencies, for instance, were actively involved in the negotiations as well. Ambassadors from Pakistan, Iran, and Egypt were also reluctantly permitted to be there by President Jimmy

Carter. Though gravely concerned that the ambassadors would be a prime target for the terrorists, Carter also felt that they could help negotiate a peaceful end to the crisis.

Nonetheless, the D.C. department led by Cully took the lead in working with the terrorists to negotiate that peaceful end.

"I absolutely had none of the problems that people would generally assume you would have," Cully would say after the incident. "Everybody deferred to the department's judgment. There was no attempt on anybody's part to take it over. Maybe nobody else wanted it."

The first thing Cully did was to deny the terrorists their demand to release the killers of the Khaalis family. This set a firm boundary with Khaalis early on that Cully refused to budge from no matter how many times Khaalis demanded otherwise.

Meanwhile, the ambassadors spoke with Khaalis under Cully's supervision. They read the Quran with him in an effort to appeal to his religious values.

Cully even set down the revolver he always carried on his gun belt and went to go meet with Khaalis one-on-one in the foyer room of the B'nai B'rith room. The hostages were being held seven floors above.

In essence, Cully was attempting to do two things at once: 1. Set a firm boundary with Khaalis that he refused to budge from, and 2. Appeal to Khaalis' conscience so he wouldn't do anything violent against the hostages.

One person had already been killed and two more wounded, so Cully knew that Khaalis was very violent.

After 38 hours of deliberating, both parties were exhausted. Cully finally cut a deal with Khaalis: he would be arrested, but he would be set free on bail to await his trial.

While the deal drew criticism at the time for being too generous to the hostage takers, Cully insisted that it was the only way to bring a peaceful end to the standoff without further violence to anyone else.

Khaalis was arrested, convicted, and later died in prison in 2003. His associates were each convicted as well.

****

Two years after the incident, Cully was forced into early retirement when a demonstrator against the Vietnam War struck his knee with a brick. Many believed that it was much too soon for Cully to retire, but the impression he left on the D.C. police force would be felt for years to come.

Cully passed away from a stroke in March 2023 at the age of 90. His tenure as the D.C. police chief was looked back on fondly by police departments across the country. His role in helping to negotiate an end to the 1977 Hanafi Siege remains one of the most studied events during his time on the force.

"He was the kind of cop that was approachable," said Charles H. Ramsey, who was D.C.'s police chief from 1998 to 2006. "He is learning to talk to that boy [referencing a famous photo of Cully in which he stooped to speak to a small boy] - that was real. It showed how one viewed police and how police viewed their role. And that is having a good relationship with the people we serve."

CHAPTER SEVENTEEN

BRACK MILLER

Action movies and shows involving cops and robbers will almost always include a high-speed getaway chase and a shootout. It's almost to the point that when we think of 'cops and robbers,' we often think of a bank robbery followed by a chase and a shootout.

But it's also easy to think that incidents like these are relegated to the realm of Hollywood fiction and don't actually happen in real life. The truth, however, is that high-speed chases and gunfights between cops and robbers getting away from the scene of the robbery do sometimes occur.

We'll see this soon in the story of Brack Miller.

****

In early April 2022, it was just another day on the job for Miller, an Oklahoma Highway Patrol Officer. He was driving his police SUV along the road when he was suddenly notified of an armed robbery suspect who was driving a black SUV at a fast speed.

Troopers had already asked the suspect to come to a halt at a traffic stop, but when he instead accelerated his vehicle, a high-speed pursuit began.

The suspect was Charles Carswell, a man who was suspected of a robbery in Arizona and was now attempting to flee across Oklahoma.

Miller caught sight of Carswell in the black SUV and began his pursuit. Seeing Miller's police cruiser with his flashing lights coming up on him, Carswell pushed down hard on the gas pedal.

Miller likewise pushed down on his own pedal, and soon the two SUVs were racing past the other vehicles on the road. Miller held on tight to his steering wheel as he maintained focus on Carswell's vehicle and provided steady updates to his fellow officers via his radio.

Suddenly, shots rang out and smashed through Miller's front window, missing him by inches! Carswell was shooting from the driver's seat in his vehicle, and the bullets had shot out of the rear window of his car.

The gunfire did nothing to deter Miller. If Carswell thought it would get Miller to break off the chase or swerve his vehicle out of control, he was quickly proven wrong.

Miller's vehicle came up on the rear of Carswell's. Miller attempted to perform a PIT, where a pursuing vehicle will hit the rear side of a fleeing vehicle to force it to abruptly turn at 180 degrees.

Miller's first attempt to perform this maneuver failed as Carswell quickly regained control of his vehicle and continued to speed away. Initially slowed by the attempted PIT, Miller increased his speed and came up on Carswell again.

More shots exploded out the rear window of Carswell's vehicle and smashed through Miller's front windshield, again missing him by inches!

It was a miracle Miller wasn't hit. He stayed calm and collected and continued to report updates almost casually on his radio.

Miller came up on the rear of Carswell's SUV to try the PIT maneuver again, only with the same results as before.

Again, Carswell accelerated away, as if he would get away. But again, Miller slammed down on the gas pedal while holding tight onto his steering wheel. Miller was determined to end the chase, and his previous failures at the PIT maneuver or Carswell's gunfire were not going to stop him.

Coming up on the right side of Carswell's vehicle for the third time, Miller turned left, so the left front of his vehicle struck against the rear right side of Carswell. This time, the tactic worked.

Carswell lost complete control of his vehicle as his SUV swerved over 180 degrees until it was nearly sideways.

"TVI! TVI! TVI!" Miller shouted into his radio, meaning a 'Tactical Vehicle Intervention' had brought the chase to a halt.

Carswell's SUV stopped off the side of the road. Miller brought his cruiser to a standstill and exited it.

More police vehicles arrived on the scene and surrounded Carswell as he withdrew an AK-47 semi-automatic rifle and took cover behind his vehicle.

Gunfire erupted, and Carswell was hit. He later died on the scene.

****

The story of Brack Miller chasing down a robbery suspect in a high-speed pursuit is more than just a reminder that cop-and-robber car chases happen in real life.

It's also a reminder of how calm a police officer needs to remain no matter how intense the circumstances in which they find themselves.

Even though Miller was chasing down a suspect at high speeds and taking incoming gunfire through his front window that barely missed him, he never lost focus, allowed his vehicle to swerve out of control, or stopped providing updates to his officers through his radio. And even though his first two PIT attempts to stop Carswell failed, Miller refused to give up on the chase and kept trying again and again until he succeeded.

Miller acted exactly how a police officer should act in a high-speed car chase: stay calm and focus on the fleeing suspect and have the determination never to give up.

CHAPTER EIGHTEEN

ALEXIS CALLAWAY

Police officers on duty are responsible for the safety and protection of all members of the general public whom they serve. This includes small children and infants, who often are less at risk from violent criminals than they are from themselves..., especially when it comes to choking hazards.

This is why police officers knowing how to perform CPR on infants and children is so important, especially when you consider that hundreds of children die from choking in the United States each year - and thousands more are rushed to emergency rooms.

Alexis Callaway was an SRO, or school resource officer, in Senoia, Georgia. SROs are police officers who work with school administrators on campus to help ensure a safe environment. While she spent most of her days at the school, Callaway also went out on patrol.

While on patrol one afternoon, Callaway received a call that an infant was choking in a nearby home. A family had called 911, reporting that the four-week-old baby in their house was choking and having great difficulty breathing.

As soon as she got the call, Callaway spun around her vehicle and sped toward the coordinates she had received. Arriving at the scene with another Senoia police officer, she rushed into the family's home. It was a good thing that Callaway was one of the officers who had received the call because she was both certified in CPR and had experience working with small children.

"I've been certified since the age of 16 and working with kids and stuff like that," Callaway later said.

When the officers burst inside, they found the family surrounding a grandmother holding the baby.

Callaway swiftly took the baby from the grandmother and began to apply life-saving first aid.

"No hesitation," Callaway reported later. "I saw the baby. Saw that it was the grandmother that had the baby. I took it. Made myself at home and started going."

First, Callaway inverted the baby on his side and then started patting his back. Her heart was racing fast because she could feel that the baby was not breathing - it was as if he was lifeless.

But Callaway knew that putting a baby on their side at a slightly downward angle and then patting them on their back rapidly was one of the best strategies to release anything obstructing their airway.

She had used the technique before with success, and she knew it was the best chance of survival for the small baby she now held in her arms.

Suddenly, the baby spat out some liquid. He began choking and making noises, and Callaway continued patting him on his back until he began breathing normally.

The family was immensely relieved. The grandmother took the baby back into her arms, and everyone lavished thanks and gratitude on Callaway.

****

Callaway found out from the family afterwards that the baby had been unable to swallow the liquid from his bottle, and it had somehow become blocked in his airway.

It was a miracle that she responded to the incident in time to save the baby's life. This is why it's so important for people to know how to perform CPR on infants and children, Callaway would later say in an interview. If she or another officer had not arrived on time, the baby most certainly would have lost his life. She advises all new parents of children to become CPR certified.

Callaway's heroism did not go unnoticed.

"She prevented what could have been a disastrous outcome in that even though during that time of mayhem, she just brought a sense of calm to that entire incident," said Jason Ercole, the Captain of the Senoia Police Department.

In recognition of her actions, Callaway received the Senoia Police Departments' lifesaving award later that month.

"It's rewarding," Callaway said - not about the award that she received but to the life of the baby she saved. "He was one month old, now he gets the rest of his life."

CHAPTER NINETEEN

TONI SCHUCK

Toni Schuck was a 26-year veteran of the South Florida Highway Patrol. March 22, 2022, was a beautiful Sunday morning, and Schuck was posted in her Chevrolet Tahoe police vehicle on the southbound entrance ramp that led to the Sunshine Skyway Bridge in Manatee County.

The Armed Force Skyway 10k was in full swing, and between seven to eight thousand people were gathered there and taking part in a long-distance road running competition over the bridge.

As Schuck looked on, she received an urgent radio call. A 2011 BMW sedan was driving at high speeds and headed straight for the bridge, having failed to stop for a road closure!

"At that point, I was facing northbound," Schuck recalled. "I turned my car around and faced southbound."

The driver of the BMW was 52-year-old Kristen Watts, a woman from Sarasota, and she had passed many police barricades, cones, and law enforcement officers without slowing down. She was on a collision course with the runners on the bridge!

"In my mind, I'm thinking she's going to stop," Schuck said. "We have another checkpoint that she will stop at. I also knew I was the last one, and I knew there was nobody else behind me."

In other words, if Watts drove past the final checkpoint in between her and the bridge, there would be nothing or no one who could stop her from plowing into the runners on the bridge…, no one, that is, except for Schuck.

Schuck believed that Watts would be stopped by the final checkpoint in between her BMW and the bridge, but she didn't want to take any chances. Schuck positioned her Chevrolet Tahoe in the middle of the road.

"I'm not trained to do that, it was just an instinct," Shuck said. "I thought that she would see the truck and then she would stop."

As fate would have it, Watts drove fast through the final checkpoint. She was now headed directly to the bridge with the more than 7,000 people running over it - and Schuck and her Tahoe were all that was standing in her way.

Up ahead, Schuck could now see Watts' BMW barreling down the road to the bridge at an accelerated speed. Schuck kept her Tahoe positioned in the middle of the road and began driving to meet Watts head-on.

When Watts veered left, Schuck veered left, and when Watts veered right, Schuck veered right, to ensure they would collide in the middle.

There was only one thing going through Schuck's mind: if she failed to collide directly with Watts, then her BMW would plow directly into those thousands of people on the bridge and cause casualties on a mass scale.

"The next thing was the crash," Schuck recalled. "It's hard because I've done this for 26 years, and I've never been in this position…, where I've had to put myself on the line for somebody else."

The two vehicles collided head-on with one another, stopping Watts' BMW directly in its tracks.

Both women sustained injuries from the collision, but Schuck was in far worse condition. More police officers and medical emergency first responders soon arrived on the scene. Schuck was carefully removed from the vehicle and placed into an ambulance.

As the ambulance crossed back over the Sunshine Skyway Bridge, she saw the runners on the road. They had stopped and were waving at her. They had seen what had happened and knew what Schuck had done to protect them. Schuck was overwhelmed with emotion.

****

"Every day since it happened, I've thought about it," Schuck recalled. "You go through the what-ifs. But I was the last officer. I knew that. I knew it was me. So, if it wasn't me to get her to stop, then who?"

Six hours after she was arrested, Watts tested well above the legal intoxication limit. She would be charged with a DUI with serious injury, two counts of DIY with property damage, and two counts of reckless driving that involved injury and property damage. However, investigators did not believe that Watts was intentionally trying to harm the runners. Instead, she was just so impaired she did not have any regard for pedestrians or other vehicles on the road.

The spokesman for the Skyway 10k used the final marketing conference for the event to bring attention and praise to Schuck's action. He presented Schuck with a customized race bib with her badge number on it.

"It's heroic in every aspect of the word," said Judge at the conference, "at that point, there were still probably a couple of thousand people on the bridge. A lot of those folks are also law enforcement members or their family members are in law enforcement. Our gratitude is extreme."

At a ceremony later that year, the commissioners of Manatee County presented Schuck with the 2022 Florida Highway Patrol Officer of the Year Award.

"You showed such courage and bravery," said Vanessa Baugh, the Manatee County Commissioner at the ceremony, "I just thank you from the bottom of my heart for what you did."

Kevin Van Ostenbridge, the Commission Chair for Manatee County, echoed Baugh's sentiment, saying, "Trooper Schuck's quick thinking and selfless decision to risk her life diverted a lethal disaster."

The commissioners further honored Schuck by marking March 22, 2022, as Toni Schuck Day.

CHAPTER TWENTY

ANNETTE GOODYEAR

It was a rainy day on February 8, 2022, in Cecil County, Maryland. North East Police Department Corporal Annette Goodyear was dressed in a bright orange poncho and was helping guide children over a crosswalk on their way to school.

One girl was about to cross the road when Goodyear spotted a black sedan coming at a high speed toward the crosswalk. As the girl was crossing the road, Goodyear held up her arm, indicating for the vehicle to stop.

The girl was already crossing the middle of the sidewalk, and the sedan wasn't slowing down, so Goodyear stepped up to position herself between the car and the girl.

As the car closed in, Goodyear could see it wasn't going to stop. Thinking quickly, she grabbed the girl by her shoulders and shoved her out of the way just as the sedan slammed into Goodyear!

Goodyear was flung from her feet and hard to the pavement. She attempted to get up but was so stunned by the blow of the car that she sank back to the ground.

The car came to a halt, and the driver ran out of the car and came to Goodyear's aid. The student Goodyear had saved and multiple onlookers ran over to surround Goodyear as well.

Goodyear's first concern after being hit was not for herself but for the student.

She would later say: "I just remember laying on the ground and looking up, and the first thing I thought was 'Where is the student'?"

But Goodyear was still too stunned to physically get up and check on her.

"I felt horrible," Goodyear would say, "because I couldn't just jump up and grab a hold of her and say 'everything is okay'."

Miraculously, Goodyear only sustained minor injuries and was released shortly after being taken to the hospital. She was also immensely glad to hear that the child she had pushed out of the way had not sustained any injuries.

"Everything just happened so quickly," Goodyear later recalled. "It just didn't seem real."

****

The incident gained the attention of then-Maryland Governor Larry Hogan.

"Like so many Marylanders, I was moved by the video of Corporal Annette Goodyear selflessly putting herself in harm's way to save a young student from being hit by an oncoming car."

"We're just extremely proud of her actions," said Corporal Jon Fakner from the same department. "It was a split-second reaction that saved a child from potential injury. A job well done."

The driver who hit Goodyear was issued four traffic citations for negligent driving, driving on an expired registration plate, failing to stop at a pedestrian in a crosswalk, and failing to stop at a yield sign before entering the crosswalk.

Goodyear claimed her quick thinking and decisiveness in the situation were because she was a mother of three. She couldn't imagine the immense pain that she would feel if a car struck one of her children while they were merely trying to go to school. When Goodyear saw the young girl crossing the street and the black sedan coming racing down, the only thing she could think about was how that child's parents would feel in the event of a serious accident.

Goodyear did what any police officer should do and put herself in harm's way to protect the life of a member of the public - and she did it with quick thinking and without any concern for her own safety or well-being.

"This is a kid, and I'm an adult," Goodyear said, "no matter what happens, you've got to protect that child and make sure that child is safe. That was the only thing going through my mind. If I have to take the brunt of it, that's what's going to happen.

Goodyear's concern for the student did not end after the accident. When she was released from the hospital, Goodyear immediately drove down to the girl's home to check up on her.

Upon seeing Goodyear enter the house, the girl burst into tears and ran up to Goodyear and hugged her. The girl's father became teary-eyed as well.

Governor Hogan recognized Goodyear's actions by publicly awarding her a governor's citation for putting herself at risk to save the student's life.

An executive of Cecil County, Danielle Hornberger, publicly praised Goodyear as well.

"It was an amazing act of heroism,' Hornberger said. "It's breathtaking, it's amazing, and we're just so proud to have Corporal Goodyear in our community."

CONCLUSION

Law enforcement departments all over the world are often embroiled in controversy for a variety of reasons, whether it be corruption within a department or incidents of police officers overextending beyond their legal reach or using excessive force.

Unfortunately, it's these kinds of negative incidents involving law enforcement that can attract the highest number of media and public attention, and it can subsequently paint law enforcement as a whole in a rather unfavorable light. This can overshadow the work of police officers serving who work tirelessly and courageously to help keep us safe.

That's why it's also vitally important to remember that there are many police officers, both retired and currently on duty, who are among the most heroic and respectable people in our society today. The 20 individuals who we have discussed in this book represent only a very small fraction of all the heroic law enforcement officers who have served with courage.

One of the fundamental duties of a police officer is to help maintain law and order and to protect people in the general public from harm.

That being said, the work of a police officer can, admittedly, be very mundane and monotonous, from handing out parking or speeding tickets to doing paperwork at a desk. But the police officer must always be ready, on a moment's notice, to put their lives on the line to protect members of the public and to act with the right combination of bravery and decisiveness.

That's exactly what we've seen in these 20 real-life stories. Every single one of these police officers was forced into a situation without warning where they put their own life at risk to protect the lives of other people.

Look at Rajkamal Meena when he dived into the cold river to save the boy from drowning, despite not knowing how to swim well. Or Michael Gregorek or Donald Thompson who pushed themselves through the windows of burning vehicles to save the lives of innocents trapped inside. Or

Terrance Yeakey who ran into a blown-up building on the verge of collapse to carry injured people to safety.

What's more, police officers often have to go up against numerous assailants or criminals alone, or against an assailant or criminal who may be physically larger and likelier to win a one-on-one confrontation.

Look at Clare Chambers who went up against a violent man much larger than she was, or Wayne Marques who took on three terrorists armed with knives at once to stop them from killing or hurting other people.

Not every police officer who serves will have to risk their life to save the lives of others like we've talked about in this book. But every police officer has to be prepared to do so.

The next time you see a police officer standing in line at the coffee shop or grocery store, consider taking a moment to thank them to show your appreciation. The time that officer may be called upon to act to save the life of another may be fast approaching.

www.ingramcontent.com/pod-product-compliance
Lightning Source LLC
Chambersburg PA
CBHW060229030426
42335CB00014B/1381